The Making of a
KING

Despite the Challenges In Life

Benjamin Osei Kuffour Jnr.

Copyright © 2016. All rights reserved.

No part of this publication may be reproduced, stored in a retrieval system or transmitted in any way by any means, electronic, mechanical, photocopy, recording or otherwise, without the prior permission of the author except as provided by USA copyright law.

All characters appearing in this work are fictitious. Any resemblance to real persons, living or dead, is purely coincidental.

The opinions expressed by the author are not necessarily those of Revival Waves of Glory Books & Publishing.

Published by Revival Waves of Glory Books & Publishing

PO Box 596| Litchfield, Illinois 62056 USA

www.revivalwavesofgloryministries.com

Revival Waves of Glory Books & Publishing is committed to excellence in the publishing industry.

Book design Copyright © 2016 by Revival Waves of Glory Books & Publishing. All rights reserved.

Published in the United States of America

Paperback: 978-1-68411-046-9

Table of Contents

CHAPTER ONE - CHOSEN 4

CHAPTER TWO – GOLIATH 26

CHAPTER THREE – IN THE PALACE 50

CHAPTER FOUR – WILDERNESS LIFE 73

CHAPTER FIVE – DEALING WITH ENEMIES 94

CHAPTER SIX – FACING SETBACKS 117

CHAPTER SEVEN – ON THE THRONE 122

Also Available By Benjamin Osei Kuffour Jnr. 142

CHAPTER ONE - CHOSEN

I am going to consider the life of a gentleman who was elevated from a very low level to a very high level. His name is David. I am going to do a study on the life of David up to when he became king. I will not delve into his life as king, but rather at the making of a king; how he was lifted up from the backside of the desert, a simple shepherd boy who rose up to the highest level.

I believe God can also raise you up to a very high level. This teaching is going to help you identify the various phases that God is taking you through as He raises you to a high level.

The main text is going to be from 1 Samuel 16:1-13.

Verse 1, *"Now the Lord said to Samuel, 'How long will you mourn for Saul, seeing I have rejected him from reigning over Israel? Fill your horn with oil and go. I am sending you to Jesse, the Bethlehemite, for I have provided myself a king among his sons.'"*

If you know a bit about the background of the story, the first king of Israel was Saul. Saul was elevated, but he could not really handle the position well and so he lost God's favor. Now God is choosing the next king and He instructs Samuel on the process for choosing the next king.

Verse 4, *"So Samuel did what the Lord said and went to Bethlehem and the elders of the town trembled at his coming and said, 'Do you come peaceably?' and he said, 'Peaceably. I have come to sacrifice to the Lord. Sanctify yourselves and come with me to the sacrifice.' Then he consecrated Jesse and his sons and invited them to the sacrifice. So it was when they came, that he looked at Eliab and said, 'Surely the Lord's anointed is before him.' But the Lord said to Samuel, 'Do not look at his appearance or at his physical stature because I have refused him. For the Lord does not see as man sees. For man looks at the outward appearance, but the Lord looks at the heart.' "*

Verses 11-13, *"And Samuel said to Jesse, 'Are all the young men here?' then he said, 'There remains yet the youngest and there he is, keeping the sheep.' And Samuel said to Jesse, 'Send and bring him. For we will not sit down until he comes here. So he sent and brought him in. Now he was ready with bright eyes and good looking and the Lord said, 'Arise, anoint him, for this is the One.' Then Samuel took the horn of oil, anointed him in the midst of his brothers and the Spirit of the Lord came upon David from that day forward. So Samuel arose and went to Ramah.' "*

God wants to elevate somebody. God wants to raise somebody to the place of kingship in Israel and He chooses a very little town, Bethlehem, and a family in Bethlehem headed by a man called Jesse who has several sons at least from this indication, eight sons in all.

Samuel comes to the house of Jesse. He goes through the process of consecration, prepares them, for God to determine whom He has chosen and they start from the oldest boy, Eliab. He obviously is a very confident young man and Eliab comes in front of Samuel; he has the stature, he has the physical properties. Everything around him smells like a king and Samuel presumes that this is the king. He actually says to himself, "Behold, The Lord's anointed is before Him" because Eliab looked kingly. He had the physical presence of a king. I am sure he was tall, muscular, carried himself with confidence because if you are a first born, you tend to be very confident. He carried himself with confidence and I am sure he spoke with a sufficiently deep voice and so when he strode before Samuel he looked like a king.

Remember that the king who had just been rejected was Saul and Saul himself was a very tall, imposing figure. Saul was the kind of person that you saw and felt, "This must just be a king." And so Samuel, with that experience of Saul, saw Eliab and thought, "This must be the king." God said, "No. No. This is not the one. I have refused him. This is not the one I have chosen." And so the rest of the boys come in – seven of them. They ended the cycle and none of them is chosen. So Samuel says, "God is not wrong. There must be something left here."

There is **an eighth born**. Eight is always **the number of new beginnings.** Eighth born and he is the youngest. He is out there taking care of sheep and Samuel said, "If it is not these seven, it must be the number eight." So he said, "We will wait for him. We will not sit till he comes." David comes in, and immediately the Holy Spirit says to Samuel, "This is the one."

I am going to consider aspects about David that predisposed him towards God's election. When we are introduced to David in this passage, there are **three facts** we are introduced to concerning David.

The first fact we will notice about David is **his position in the family**. He is described as the youngest. That means he was small in size, and less in ranking. Not just young in age but he was also the smallest in size. In terms of family order, he was the least. He was the one who had the least power, the least ranking, the person you will not think of immediately as king. So in position, he was small and he was least in rank.

Secondly, we are introduced to **David's priorities**. What were his priorities? He was the keeper of the sheep – the sheep of the family. Is it not amazing that there were older boys who were available for selection but were not available for work? When it was time for them to be promoted all of them showed up and you wonder, "What were they doing previously?" They were obviously just loitering about, doing nothing. But David has different priorities. He is the keeper of the sheep. The word keeper means he associated with the sheep, he fed the sheep, he guided the sheep and he protected the sheep. So considering his priority, David is not looking for post. He is looking for work. He is not interested in who is the oldest, who is the next king. He is just doing his job – taking care of the sheep. He has a commitment to his work. He watches the sheep. He secures the sheep. He feeds the sheep. So his priorities are right.

Thirdly, you are introduced to **the personality of David**. His position, his priorities, his personality. The Bible describes him as "ruddy, bright eyed and good looking." All these descriptions paint one picture. Ruddy means that he was "red." Why was he red? The sun had beat so hard on him his skin had been red. He was exposed to trouble, pain, difficulty, but in spite of that, he had "good eyes." In ancient Israel when they said someone had good eyes, it meant that the person was handsome. He has good eyes. That is why the Bible said Lea's eyes, the one Jacob wanted to marry, were not good. Her eyes were weak because in ancient Israel that is how they described beauty. A person who is good looking has good eyes. In Ghana, in most of the languages, when a person is beautiful, we literally say, "The skin is nice." Is that not so? "Ne ho ye fe." That is how we describe beauty. The skin is nice. In ancient Israel, the eyes are good, but the phrase good looking means that he had a good attitude about himself. You see he has a smile on his face and he is very confident about what he is doing; just a good person to hang around with. That is how David was.

Now, it is very interesting that both David and Eliab are described in physical terms, but God rejects one and accepts the other because Eliab is also a man of good stature. David is also handsome. So how come both of them have good physical properties, but God rejects one and takes the other? I believe the reason is because Eliab was arrogant in his physical strength; the kind of person who knows he looks good and wants everybody to know he feels good and when he is walking by, he is checking at the corner of his eye to find out who is watching him. He is the kind of person who goes to his friends and says, "Were they looking at me?"

He calls attention to himself because he was the first born. He believes that he must have the best and he has the first bourn's confidence. It is the kind of confidence you hear during beauty pageant events. Ladies during this time praised themselves highly, calling attention to themselves about how they look. "I am elegant. I am eloquent. I am beautiful. I am bold. I am that."

If you go and do that before God, He will fail you. Man may be impressed with that. That is why the Bible says, "Man looks on the outward." If you go to God and say, "God, look at me. Check me out, Father. What do you think? You did a good job on me. Check me." He will check you, but He will check you wrong. David is also handsome, good looking, but it is not important to Him. Have you met people who have what it takes but they act as if it is nothing? That is how David was. He was handsome, had bright eyes, but it was secondary to Him because what was more important to Him was his heart, not his physical structure.

Some of you have been blessed by God physically and you think that entitles you to greatness in life. I have some good news for you that God's criteria does not include pride and arrogance and if you come with that before God, you will fail even before the question paper is brought out. David had a good personality. He is bright eyed, he is handsome and he has gone through serious toughness. He stands before Samuel and something about him, definitely, not his appearance because God looks in the heart; something about him just registers on God's list and He is chosen.

In this passage, there are **two important people** I want to introduce to you. I call them David's Two Fathers. David has two fathers because they are crucial to your elevation and promotion in life.

The first one that most of us are familiar with is **Jesse, the natural father of David. He is the one who gave birth to David**. He is the one David is usually associated with – Jesse. Under Jesse, David's chances in life were determined by natural order. Under Jesse, if David was going to be great, then he had to follow the natural order and if you look at how Jesse does it, the first born comes, the second born comes, the third and down and down and down. By the time it gets to David, all hope is lost because in Jesse's mind if the first born did not make it, how can he make it? That is how Jesse is thinking because Jesse says, "The older the first, the youngest last." So if David was going to be successful, under his father's system, then he had to wait for a long queue of successful people before it gets to his turn. **Jesse represents the natural order**.

Secondly, **Jesse represents uncertain heritage**. The heritage of David under Jesse was uncertain. It was not sure. It was not clear. He could not tell where his future lay. So under that system, the natural system, there is uncertainty. You cannot be sure, and some of us if we look at the natural order and our natural parentage – our heritage is very uncertain. Definitely, if you cannot say it for yourself, I can say it for myself.

Thirdly, under Jesse, **David was overlooked and abandoned**. If you work according to the natural, people will overlook you because you are too skinny. You are too thin. You are too short. You are not well-educated. Your brothers are smarter than you. Let me tell you that there is no equality anywhere in this world, not even in a family. Some children will be first, others will be the last born of the same parents. It works that way. The parents' natural attitude will be that the child who is first in class will be first in life and sometimes some parents actually begin to praise the one who performs in class and begins to disgrace the one who performs least because according to their perking order, the natural order, you have no way of succeeding due to the fact that you were bad in class. That is, under Jesse. David was abandoned and overlooked because he was small and he was low on the perking order.

Can you imagine, what it was for that young boy, the eighth born, to be in the field all by himself? Nobody visited him. Nobody even went to whisper to him, "Listen. Something has happened in the family. Samuel, the great prophet, has come to our house." Just for him to see Samuel. Nobody told him. Can you imagine? It is like the President of Ghana comes to visit you and your parents do not bother to call the whole family to come and see the President and take a picture with him. He is overlooked. He does not matter. We do not know why he is overlooked, but he is overlooked and abandoned.

Fourthly, under Jesse, **he is the least, likely to succeed**. Everything went against David. It is believed that his mother was not even the "Mrs." His mother was somebody else, not the "Mrs." David himself said, "In sin, did my mother conceive me." So the mother was a young girl in the neighborhood who tempted Jesse or whom Jesse tempted but there was a temptation somewhere. An old man running after a young girl in the neighborhood and so she gives birth to this last born who is too young and she is not the Mrs. Nobody knows how to deal with him because he is a problem child. He creates trouble when he comes around. Jesse does not know how to handle David. He is the least likely to succeed. If you asked Jesse to choose one of his children to be successful, he will not pick David because he is trouble in the family. So the best way to manage David is to keep him away out there keeping the sheep.

In Ghana, sometimes the best way to handle a David is to let him go live with an uncle or aunt or put him somewhere else that he cannot always show up because anytime he shows up Mrs. is angry. So we have to make sure Mrs. does not see this child. He is abandoned, overlooked and he is kept out of harm's way. If you look at his chances of success, they are not very bright.

He is the least likely, but in the midst of that, God brings another father to David. He is called Samuel. Samuel is not a physical father; he is a spiritual father and he comes to change the options available for David because God will always bring a Samuel your way between you and your throne, between you and your destiny, between you and where God wants you to get to. If your natural order does not help you, God will bring you a Samuel. He is not related to you by blood. He is not your blood relation. He is not your uncle, but he is somebody with a new mandate on your life and Samuel comes in as a spiritual father and under Samuel, David is now on God's divine order. He is no longer on the natural order and as you know, in God's divine order, God messes up the whole hierarchy.

Esau, Jacob, bless one. Once you get into God's order, you cannot tell what is going to happen. He picks Jacob and leaves the first born. Manasseh, Ephraim, bless one. He crosses the hand. In God's order, the last becomes the first and so Samuel introduces David to God's order. Samuel is literally saying you are the least of your family, but when you come into God's order, He changes the whole system and then you have the chance of success in your life.

Under Samuel, there is a sure inheritance. It is no longer uncertain. It is no longer tentative. It is sure. It is clear. David has an inheritance with God. Under Samuel, David, who is abandoned and overlooked is now known and called. "Is there not another one? We will not sit down until he comes."

I am sure the whole family is troubled. It is almost like a Cinderella story. The family is troubled. The troublesome child, the problem child, we are trying to manage out there, the prophet comes to town and is looking for him and the prophet actually says, "We will not sit down." Literally meaning, we will stand and wait for him, giving him high value and importance.

He is now known and now called. Under Samuel, David is divinely favored to succeed. Under Jesse, he is the least likely to succeed. At a certain point in your life, God is going to introduce a Samuel into your life. Maybe your pastor, who comes to you and begins to speak new words to you that are totally different from the words you heard when you were growing up. Everything you heard was that you were at the bottom, you were dumb, you will not amount to anything and you cannot do it and you are troublesome. Everything you heard programmed you for failure. Then you go somewhere else and someone begins to speak new words into your life and those words are totally opposite. Everything you have heard. That is the role of a Samuel. The Samuel comes and introduces a prophetic Word of God into your life. It may not be a prophetic Word that says, "I am the Lord! I am the Lord!! I have called you. I have chosen you." No. It may be just a Word from the pulpit. It may be a Word from a CD. It may be a Word from a DVD. It may be a Word from a book, but you read it and all of a sudden, everything you believe was impossible in your life now appears possible. That is the role of a Samuel. He changes the order and when Samuel comes into your life he also tells you your future is certain. You have a choice to make, either you are going to obey the pull of Samuel or the pull of Jesse.

Jesse is pulling you, Samuel too is pulling you. Jesse pulls you backwards; Samuel pulls you forward and you have to determine at a point where you are going to flow. You can either flow with Jesse or you flow with Samuel. For David, that day he determined whom his future lay with. It no longer lay with Jesse. It now lay with Samuel. This is where God wants me to be.

If I look at myself naturally, I can never get to this point, but if I look at what God is telling me now, I can get to that point. You have a choice to make, either to go by the pull of your past or the pull of your future. At every point in time, your future is speaking to you and your past is also speaking to you. Your past is calling you to what you have done, your future is calling you to what you can do.

Your past is calling you to your performance. Your future is calling you to your potential. Your past is reminding you of your failures. Your future is reminding you of what can be done through the grace of God and you have to choose where to go to. I do not know what you have done with your life. Maybe you have messed up your life big time. You have messed up your life ten times over and when you think about your own life, you cry for yourself. You feel sad for yourself because you have made some terrible mistakes you do not think you can forgive yourself.

That is Jesse but at the same time, God brings a Samuel. Samuel says, "David, your mother may not have done the right thing. She may have conceived you out of wedlock. Your father played the truant but God still has a plan and purpose for you. Which one are you going to go by? Are you going to go by Jesse or Samuel? " These are the two fathers.

God will always bring you those fathers. When Samuel came into the life of this young boy, everything changed because he somehow fitted into God's expectation. God's viewpoint in appointing a leader or raising people into leadership is based on the heart. God does not look at your outward manifestation. He looks at your heart. He looks at your heart. That is how God looks at things. If God was to choose Miss Ghana, the person God will choose will be different from the one everybody voted for or texted for because you are impressed with the person who says, "Vote for me. I am the most beautiful." You look at her and some men begin to lust after her and you text. Your fantasies are aroused.

God will not say when He comes, "I want to see how you dance." Or "Wear a bikini before I choose you." God will not say, "I want to see whether you speak English too well and perfectly." God will say, "I want to see your heart." If your heart is right, I will take you there because the man looks at things totally different from God. You may not have all the physical attributes, but if your heart is in the right place, you are on God's agenda to be chosen. So what does it mean when God says, "He looks to the heart."?

There are **four reasons**. Normally, your heart is used **for your attitude, but four facts to define your heart.**

Your affections. Your values. The things that are important to you. For David, God is looking for a shepherd over his people and he sees this boy who is shepherding sheep and God says, "If this boy has so much affection for sheep which cannot talk back to him, I can trust him to shepherd my people Israel. He risks his life for the sheep. He sleeps with them. He protects them. He feeds them. He does not get anything back. He is not paid for doing it because the money goes to his father and Eliab will get all the money. He is not doing it for the salary. He is doing it because he loves it. That is where your heart is. The things you love.

These days, people want to be paid for everything. People do not know how to do things from a pure heart to say, "Listen… just… it is ok. Just doing it from my heart." Every little thing they want a little money and that is all you will get.

Little money and people who pursue little money for every little service, never amount to anything great because their affections are wrong. God looks to the heart.

Secondly, the heart talks about **your emotions**. Your passions. The things you are passionate about and if you know anything about David, he was passionate for the presence of God. He was passionate for God. He will sit in those dark nights with his sheep and take his harp and begin to play and begin to worship God and begin to encourage himself although he was alone. Nobody was there, he had offered pure worship to God.

One of those Psalms he wrote in those moments, we still quote it, the most popular, "The Lord is my shepherd. I shall not want." And he goes on and on. He begins to praise God. He is not complaining. He is not planning how to avenge his brothers. He is not planning on how he will show his brothers when God lifts him up. He is just passionate for God. Where are your emotions? Are your emotions full of anger, bitterness, jealousy, and envy or full of love and worship? Where is your heart because if your heart is jealous or envious, you see people who are successful, you feel bad, angry and you want to destroy them. You see somebody who is rich, whom you do not know, you start criticizing him.

"He thinks he is on top." Your heart is wrong. God looks to the heart. Your emotions. Your passions. Where is your heart? Unfortunately, a lot of us, our hearts are full of bitterness and jealousy; too much of it. There is no room for God. Too much bitterness, too much envy, too much jealousy, too much backbiting, too much trying to destroy somebody. So God comes for inspection, looks at your heart, it is full of junk.

He wants to choose you. He wants to elevate you, but your heart is wrong. David was a man of immense gratitude.

Talk about gratitude, probably he is the most grateful person you will ever find in the Scriptures. A person who knows how to show gratitude for good deeds that has been done for him. If your heart is full of ingratitude, you are not on God's list for promotion. Man may promote you, but God will never promote you and when man promotes you to a place God has not promoted you to, there will be a demotion. That is why sometimes people rise very high and fall very deep because they can impress man. You can impress a man with your speech. You can impress a man with your certificate. You can impress a man with good speeches. You can impress a man with how you look, how you walk, how you talk. You can impress man with all of that, but if God did not put you there, you will be a liability to yourself and to everybody around you. You will be a hazard to nature.

The heart also refers to **the intellect**. Your mindset. How you think. How you process ideas. How do you think? Are you negative or positive? Are you optimistic or pessimistic? Are you can-do or can-never-do? How do you think? Are you a critic or a doer? Intellect – the way you use your mind.

The heart finally refers to **your courage**. Your strength. The moral and ethical strength. When we say someone has got heart, we mean the person is courageous. The Bible says, "God looked at that. God looked at the heart." Now, how do we know that? David later on we get to know, had to fight lions to deliver a lamb. Let us face it. Let us be honest, brutally honest. If a lion comes to take a little lamb from your sheepfold, and you have several sheep, is not your last but one of the many which has been born, the lion comes to take it; the lion is running away with it.

Let us be honest, how many of you, me included, will run after the lion? Truth is, the moment we saw the lion, we will go and hide and say, "Lion, listen they are there. Take what you like." "Oh, it does not matter. One day we will kill them." But you see courage. He lays down his life for a lamb, which is not equivalent to a human life and he is fighting a lion to save a lamb. It is called courage. God looks at that heart and says, "If I need somebody to face the enemies of Israel, I need this boy. I see his heart." Eliab may look big, but when Goliath shows up, he is going to run, but this boy, David, he does not know how to run. He will fight and fight and fight even to his own peril. God says, "That is the heart I am looking for." What are you ready to fight for? Are you one of those who runs away when trouble strikes?

Your best friend has a problem and you abandon him because these days, you have to be careful especially those of you who are political. What if your best friend is for NPP and you are for the NDC, and your party is attacking your best friend and you say, "Oh, we were just mates in the same school in the same dormitory but when we were in school, this boy was a stubborn."

If you want to have the heart, then you say, "My friend is my friend and if you fight him, I will stand with him and if you want to fight me with him, then fight me also and if I am going to die, I will die also. Then God looks at that heart, "I need a courageous person and you qualify."

People do not rise into leadership for nothing. Cowards never rise into leadership. People with no value system, with no backbone who bend under every pressure never amount to any greatness and for us, mostly Ghanaians, who like saving our beautiful skin, we will deny everybody including our mother. "Oh, she says she is my mother. Hmmm they used to say that but they said she was not really my true mother." You will sell your mother because most of us have no value system. We only protect our interests.

If it does not favor us, we will sacrifice anything and everybody. Do you have courage? Can you stand for what you believe in? If you were threatened, will you stand firm? Will you protect somebody else? Will you fight for somebody else? Will you stand with somebody else? If people in authority threaten you, will you abandon what you believe in? God looks to the heart. What is He looking for? Courage. He is looking for your passions, your affections, how you think - your mindset, your intellect, how you process information, how you see life.

God looks at all of that and He says, "That boy will do it." Later on, as we study the life of David, I do not know anybody who qualifies the way he qualified. No wonder, God says, "This is the man after my heart." A man whose priorities are right, who does not use his popularity to usurp authority. If David wanted to do a coup d'états against Saul, he would have succeeded because the women were singing, "He has killed his ten thousand and Saul has only killed thousand." Only women know how to sing those songs. Can you imagine? The votes were on his side; ten thousand votes against thousand votes. The guy had the votes, not only did he have the votes, he had prophetic auction. He had been anointed and not only that, the evidence was that Saul was now demon-possessed. Now, how are you going to feel if your leader is demon-possessed, the people are for you, you have the support of the masses, what are you going to do? The easiest thing to do is to use it for your own advantage.

David looked at Saul, the man wants to kill him (David has the masses' support). The anointing, popular opinion was on his side, the military were for him, but he says, "I am not going to touch this man." If God wants to remove him, He knows how to do that and if God wants me to be a king, I am not going to kill somebody in the process of being king." No wonder God says, "I do not look to the outward. I look to the heart. There is something about this boy that impresses me, although he is number eight, I will make him number one." If you want God to elevate you, let your heart be right.

The final thing that happened to David that day was **the anointing**. David received something called the anointing – the endearment and the endowment of God's power. What does the anointing do?

First of all, **the anointing signifies God's approval**. It shows "This is the person God approves of." When your heart is right, God will approve of you.

Secondly, **the anointing separates unto a higher purpose**. He is number eight, but now he is being set aside for something bigger than his natural birthright guarantees him.

Thirdly, **the anointing sets a new direction for life**. If you want to move in a new direction, it is going to take God's anointing.

Fourthly, **the anointing stirs up your gifts and your abilities**. There are gifts in you that you have not discovered yet – latent potential. Talents you have not discovered. Abilities you have not touched yet. They are there, but either of your own background, the way you have been treated, you will never know you have those potentials, but God touches you and all of a sudden, your gifts start getting stirred up. There is going to be a stirring.

The anointing secures God's protection. When God anoints you, no one can kill you before your time because God will protect you. He has invested in you and as such He has to secure his investment. He has invested purpose in you. He will protect his investment because God lays value to what He wants you to do. You will not die until you have done it. Your life is essential to the plans and purposes of God because something about you must touch the world. When your heart is right, the world is looking for you and

God will invest the destiny of nations in your hand and you cannot die until you have fulfilled your purpose. No one can destroy a person that God has anointed until the purpose of the anointing has been accomplished.

They will cut your head, but you will still speak. Your head will be down somewhere saying, "Put me back." You will be protected in the air, on the ground, on the sea, by day, by night because God has invested in you and the anointing of David took place before his brethren. The people who taught he would not amount to much, God anoints him before them. That means no matter the jealous eyes around you, when God decides to pick on you, nobody's impression of you will stop God from doing what He wants to do. I am sure Jesse is standing somewhere saying, "Samuel, this is a mistake. It is Eliab. I groomed him for it." Eliab too is there saying, "Who does he think he is?" Everybody is hurt, "Who does he think he is?" Later on, we will realize the brothers did not repent. He is anointed. They saw the anointing, but they did not repent.

When David went to face Goliath, Eliab asked David what he was doing here. The people who do not like you, whether you are anointed or not, they do not like you. You will think, "Oh God anointed me before them; their hearts will change." You will expect from that time that they will say, "Oh David, let me wash your socks and do things for him." No. No. The anointing worsened the case. Although before them God approves of you, they will not accept you and that is why you do not have to be upset when people do not accept you contrary to every evidence that God has shown them because in David's case, that is how it happened.

If you want to be the person that God elevates this year, you want to become the king, queen in your area of endeavor, David is your example.

CHAPTER TWO – GOLIATH

As God raises you up and elevates you to the place He wants you to be, there are going to be challenges ahead of you and one of those challenges is a Goliath challenge. We are going to look at how to deal with that challenge in your life. I want to start with **two statements**:

The anointing on your life will attract significant challenges. Immediately after David was anointed, he was thrown into a situation that led him to deal with a massive challenge of his life and whenever God calls you and anoints you, He exposes you to a challenge. In the Bible, there are several instances of people who had major spiritual encounters with God and right after that were plunged into a series of conflicts, difficulties and problems.

Moses had an experience with God at the burning bush and it was a great experience, but it did not end there. It led him to confront Pharaoh. Gideon had an angelic visitation. It led him to confront the Midianite army. Esther was crowned to be queen, but she had to stand firm for her people. Jesus, immediately after His baptism, the Heavens were opened, the Spirit of God descended like a dove upon Him and the Bible says, "He was driven by the Holy Spirit to be tempted of the Devil." The moment God anoints you, the challenge of life will come your way.

Your significant challenge is equal to the calling of your life. Whatever God throws your way has a relationship with what He has called you to become. If He wants you to rise into high level of leadership, you are going to have high level problems to deal with. If you are going to function at low level leadership, you are going to have low level problems to deal with. So the higher your calling, the higher the challenge.

The size of your challenge determines the size of your reward. The bigger the problem, the bigger the pay. If you are only going to solve simple problems and you are going to be paid and rewarded in simple terms. If you are going to deal with high level reward, you have to deal with high level problems. You cannot solve low level problems and expect reward at high level. Goliath represents a high level problem because behind Goliath is a high level reward.

1 Samuel 17:3-11 is an account of this epic encounter between a young man who is still a teenager. He should be in the youth church, but he is now in adult church. He is not just dancing in the adult church. He is facing adult problems. He has to deal with problems far beyond his age, his experience and his exposure. He has never dealt with anything like this before, but it confronts him. If you want God to take you to a high level, you have to be ready for confrontations of this nature.

"The Philistines stood on a mountain on one side and Israel stood on a mountain on the other side with a valley between them.

And a champion went out from among from the camp of the Philistines, named Goliath, from Gath, whose size was six cubits and a span and he had a bronze helmet on his head and he was aimed with a coat of mail and the weight of the coat was five thousand shekels of bronze and he had bronze greaves on his legs and a bronze javelin between his shoulders.

"Now the staff of his spear was like a weaver's beam and his iron spearhead weighed six hundred shekels and a shield bearer went before him. Then he stood and cried out to the armies of Israel and said to them, 'Why have you come out to line up for battle? Am I not a Philistine? And you, the servants of Saul? Choose a man for yourselves and let him come down to me. If he is able to fight with me and kill me, then we will be your servants, but if I prevail against him and kill him, then you shall be our servants and serve us.'

And the Philistine said, 'I defy the armies of Israel this day. Give me a man that we may fight together.' When Saul and all Israel heard these words of the Philistine, they were dismayed and greatly afraid."

Goliath is real. He is not an imagination. For David, for Saul, for Israel, Goliath was a real person. He was six cubits and a span tall. A cubit is measured from the tip of your middle finger to your elbow. That is one cubit. Approximately, it is one and a half feet so one and a half feet multiplied by six is nine feet. A span is from the edge of your middle finger to your thumb. That is about nine inches. So six cubits and a span is approximately nine feet

nine inches. If you want to have an idea of what nine feet nine inches is, find someone who is six feet one inch. Goliath will be about adding half of that person who is six feet one inch on top of Goliath. That will take him very high and when he stood, he was a real human being, just the sheer size with no ammunition was enough to terrify anybody but in addition to all that, he was heavily protected.

He had bronze helmet, had a coat of mail which weighed about approximately one hundred and fifty six pounds protection. It protected his chest and his back. So the man is nine feet nine inches, helmet of bronze on his head, protected on his chest and protected from his waist down with greaves and he had a spear and a sword.

In addition to that, **he had an armor bearer in front of him**. This is an overprotected giant and he comes and what does he do? Goliath defies the authority of God. Goliath is a real challenge, for some of you, he may not be a big giant. For some of you, your Goliath is a sickness. For some people, it is a physical disability that you have to deal with. May be you were born with a physical limitation – blindness, deafness or some other form of limitation that threatens you from becoming whom God wants you to be. For some people, their Goliath may be their lack of education. It is a big problem. The anointing on them is heavy, but their education also is a limitation. That is a Goliath.

For some people, it may be a bad habit. For some people, it may be a human being who threatens you and stops you from making progress. Sooner or later, you will face a Goliath in your life and Goliath comes to tell you, "You believe you have a God. Listen to me. I defy the God who called you and if God is God, let Him fight for you." Goliath defies the authority of God. Goliath intimidates everyone else. It is a kind of problem people have which gets them intimidated and there are problems that intimidate a community, makes everybody afraid, makes everybody scared.

Thirdly, **Goliath demands a direct response**. He does not want people to fight for you. He says, "You have to fight for yourself. I just need you to fight me. Do not bring an army. Do not go hide behind your father. Do not hide behind the country. Do not hide behind the church. Do not hide behind the pastor. Face me yourself."

A Goliath challenge does not take communal labor to solve. It takes direct individual response. When Goliath faces you, he is not going to allow people to fight for you. So when you are faced with a Goliath challenge, you may be in a church, but it is your challenge alone. You may be in a family, but it is yours alone. You may have even a twin brother or sister, but Goliath does not want your twin to stand with you. You have to face Goliath by yourself. It is a direct response and if you are always depending on other people in order to feel good, Goliath will whip you out because when you face Goliath, you have to do it all by yourself.

He wants a direct response, but the good news about Goliath is that he has a high reward value. So although he is intimidating everybody else, he is defying the authority of God, he makes you feel small, he calls you to battle and you feel inadequate, the price tag on Goliath is very high and if you can deal with him, you will be happy for a very long term.

Goliath is a God-designed challenge. He is not from the Devil. God is the One who brings Goliath your way. So when you see him, it just simply means God is thinking about you for He says, "I know the thoughts that I think towards you, thoughts of good and not of evil to bring you to the expected end through Goliath." Many times, when we face a challenge, we assume it is the Devil trying to stop us, but most times when we face a challenge, it is God trying to reward you. God is seeking to honor you. God is seeking to promote you and He brings you a challenge that will necessitate an action from you that can lead to your promotion.

If God brings you little insignificant people, you can beat all of them, but nobody will recognize you. When He brings you a Goliath, just one battle, can reconfigure your destiny. Just one battle can change everything about your life. It is an epic battle. It is strategic and He is there right in your face. He is designed by God not from the Devil.

Goliath stands between you and your destiny. You want to be a king. You want to be elevated. He is going to stand between you and where God wants you to get to. Sometimes Goliath is your own bad habits. It can be a sin problem in your life. Maybe it is a sin that has destroyed everyone in your family; destroyed your fathers, your uncles, everyone – your relatives have that particular problem. It could be any problem. It could be alcoholism. It could be immorality. It could be stealing, something that destroys the reputation of your family and people around you and it is a Goliath. Whenever anyone wants to rise up, it confronts the person and destroys the person and it is now calling for you. It stands between you and your destiny and what does it do when it stands there?

He threatens your comfort. Goliath tells you that you cannot be comfortable. You cannot hide in the crowd. When I was a young boy watching war films – American and Indian – I always wondered why the Indians will rise, run in large numbers when the bullets were shot against them and they will be shot. They get shot as you watch the movie. They fall down. They just keep dying and I say to myself, "Why do they keep doing that?" If I were in the army, I will just lie down somewhere quietly before the guns come. So nobody will shoot me. I will protect myself before the battle begins. I wonder why people cannot hide in the battle and pretend they have been shot and lie down.

When you are dealing with Goliath, that option does not exist. You cannot hide in the crowd and let people fight for you. He threatens your comfort. When he comes your way, he takes away your comfort zone. You cannot be comfortable again. He will not make you sleep. He will not make you rest. He will not make you relax and if you read the Bible, the Bible says, "He will get up in the morning and he comes in the evening and for forty days he keeps going. Give me a man." Everybody is scared. Some go to sleep, praying, "Oh God, tomorrow morning, let him forget to announce his presence."

Then in the morning, they hear, "Give me a man! Give me a man!! Give a man!!!" They pray again, saying, "Oh God, let an angel strike him." The next morning, "Give me a man!" Because the battle you must fight God will not let an angel fight. "Oh God, kill him." He will not kill him. "Lord, do it for me." He will not do it for you. He says, "This is you and Goliath. I have equipped you for such a time as this."

Some of you are praying for problems that God wants you to solve and you have been praying for years and the problems are there, God says, "Enough of prayer. Get up and use weapons I have given you to confront this situation." He threatens your comfort. He taunts you with fear. He comes and mocks you, puts fear in you and makes you feel small.

Not only that, when Goliath stands between you and your destiny, **he tightens your options.** He limits your options. He does not give you space to operate. He tightens the space around you and keeps pushing you into a corner and before you realize your life has become very little because you keep running and running. One of the challenges we have in our part of the world is that from childhood we are not trained to solve personal problems. We are not trained to take charge and responsibility for our lives and as very easily as we grow up, we depend on people to take care of us. Even we are grown and are adults. We have to depend on somebody, on the extended family, on a brother and we become a dependent person.

When Goliath faces us, we want people to help us fight him, but you cannot get help. He will tighten your options. The good news about Goliath is that he is tailor-made for your strengths. He is an enemy designed specifically for you because you have what it takes to overtake him and overcome him. He is tailor-made for your strengths. Goliath was not made for Saul. Goliath was not made for Jonathan. Goliath was not made for the people in the army. Goliath was only made for one man – David. He is the reason Goliath appeared, but he had to appear before all the people to raise the price tag, so that when David appears on the scene, his training, his experience, his past, everything about David has prepared him for Goliath.

Whiles God was preparing David for Goliath, David even did not know Goliath existed, but God prepared him in a secret place waiting for the moment of opportunity to reveal the purpose of his training unto him. David knew, the moment he saw Goliath, that, "This is what I have been training for. This is what I was born to be. This man is tailor-made for me."

The Goliath in your life is not a surprise to God. God actually designed him or the situation for you because He has equipped you for what it takes to overtake that problem. He is tailor-made for your strengths.

Finally, **when Goliath stands before you, between you and your destiny, teaches you to depend on God**. As formidable as Goliath appeared, he had a weakness and that weakness was David's specialization. Goliath was nine feet nine inches tall. I am sure one step of his will probably be about two meters. He is armed, but his height, his ammunition and all the armaments he had built around him made him slow. That was the first limitation of Goliath. He seems tough, but he is slow.

Secondly, Goliath's greatest asset was **defense. His weakness was offense** because the best weapon he had was a spear and the longest a spear could go when held against an enemy will be about forty feet. The sword was for close combat. David on the other hand had only one weapon because he did not need to be close to Goliath. His specialization was a sling and a stone and he could stand four hundred feet away and accurately hit a target. So although Goliath seemed formidable, he was slow, he needed close combat and David was not going to give him close combat because everything he had been trained for was not for close combat. It was for long distance missile projected to hit a target from afar and down it before he got close to it. Thus he was tailor-made for David.

That problem you are afraid of, God designed it for you because He has been preparing you to solve such a problem in the world. He has raised the stake, so high, so when you deal with that problem, your promotion and elevation will be very fast.

There are **two ways of responding to a Goliath problem**:

Fear. That is how Saul and the rest of the army of Israel responded to Goliath. They responded in fear. Why did they respond in fear? The challenge you saw was far bigger than themselves. When you see that your problem is far bigger than you, the natural response is to fear. As a matter of fact, if you are not afraid, when your problem is far bigger than you, there must be something wrong with you. You are not normal because when your problem is bigger than you, fear comes in and that is what Israel saw. Nine feet nine inches with arms. Fear.

The second response is **faith.** How can people respond in faith? You respond in faith because God is bigger than the challenge. Fear tells you the problem is bigger than God. Faith, God is bigger than the problem. So it depends on who you trust, whether you trust in yourself or your trust in the name of the Lord. If you trust in God, it produces faith. If you trust in yourself, it is going to lead you to fear. David said, "I trust in the name of the Lord." In the battle of the words before the real, physical battle, he said to Goliath,

"You come to me with a sword and with a spear and with a shield, but I come to you in the name of the Lord, the God of Israel whose armies you have defied."

He saw God as bigger than nine feet nine inches. Many of us have no faith because we always see the problem in relation to our abilities, but never in relation to God's power. When you see it in relation to God's power, you will have faith. **How does faith respond? When you have faith, how does it respond? This is the response of faith:**

Faith prepares ahead of opportunities. Faith without works is dead. When a person has faith in what God has called him to be, he prepares himself for that moment although he has not seen the moment. Faith is the substance of things hoped for. You believe God will make you a king. In those days, the way for a person to be a king was to win battles. In those times, a king did not live in a presidential palace. Kings went to war and when they went to war, they did not stand at the back to command the people. They led the battle. Being a king in those days was a very, very, very risky job. It did not come with the election. Kings did not just spend their time having fun, waving at the crowds and shaking people and waving their party colors. No. That is not how kings function. Kings went to face enemies and if you beat them up and you conquered them, you are a king.

David had been told he would be a king. If you are going to be a king, prepare to fight even before there is an enemy. David started learning to fight even when there was no enemy. So he had to choose enemies – lions and birds in the forest. They were his enemies in the forest preparing for the real enemies later. You do not wait for opportunity before you prepare. Prepare before opportunity. Some of us are waiting for our time to come. "I am praying when my time comes..." what have you prepared for? When your time comes, can you step in to deliver the goods? Whatever you believe God has called you to be, if that opportunity came right now, will you be able to access it? Would you? Opportunity will come in a moment and opportunity only favors the prepared. It does not favor optimistic people who do not prepare. It only favors prepared people. I do not know what you believe God has called you to be but are you prepared? Are you trained? Do you have the skills? Do you have the abilities? When the challenge comes, can you overcome? Are you waiting to see the challenge before you train? If you believe in your potential, you prepare. You train. So faith responds before preparing ahead of opportunities.

Secondly, **faith recognizes the moment of history. There is a moment of history that comes everybody's way.** A moment that turns the dial of your life around. It is your moment in history. It is an opportunity and that opportunity makes all the difference. You have to recognize it. David was not even enlisted to fight that battle. His father called him, as he normally does and gave him food, provisions to go and give to his brothers and to the captain of the army of his brothers. David went with all the food, with the cheese and others, to give to the captain of the army and when he went there, he was looking for his brothers. He gave the food to the keeper of the food/provisions of the army and started walking around, whistling. I am sure he was admiring the shield and the spear and the sword and he says, "One of these days, I will be in the army. I will also be fighting and I will also hold a sword." And he is there, admiring soldiers. Then, all of a sudden, God's appointment comes on and Goliath shows up at the time David shows up.

Goliath has been making this announcement for forty days with no response, but on this fortieth day, a young boy has been sent by his father at the right time and he is out there inspecting the weapons and the ammunitions of the army, admiring the army, the king (I am sure). He is just excited to see the proud army of Israel. The bold army. The army that has won many battles. Then the giant rises, "I defy you." All of a sudden, David, looking at this army, feels so proud of running away. Can you imagine his disappointment? He comes believing in the army and everybody is running – the captains are running, people are leaving their swords behind running helter-skelter but David stands and looks on, "What is this thing that everybody is afraid of?" He hears the announcement. He sizes up the opponent. He is tall. He is big. He is slow. At that moment, something clicks in David's heart. He says, "This is what I have been training for. This is why God took me in the wilderness. This is why I was throwing stones against lions and birds. This is my moment in history. I am about to make a name for God, for my country and for myself. I am about to see the Word of God become real in my life. This is my time."

Although he was not up to the date for the enlistment to the army, he goes around and asks all these running soldiers, "Wait! Wait!! Wait!!! What will be done for the person who brings down this giant?" They say, "Well, the king says he will give his daughter to the person." Wow. "And his family will not pay taxes again." Oh yeah. The man is handsome, but poor. Left to him, he will not get the kind of wife he wants, but now the wife is available and the money is available. Whiles he is talking, his older brother comes and says, "Shut up, you insolent boy. I know the pride of your heart. You are just coming here to witness the war and go and brag that you have seen the army. Get out of here. Go home."

This is the brother who just saw David anointed, but has no value for anointing or an ointment or ointment. David responds to his brother, saying, "What have I done? All of you are running from this giant. I am asking about how to deal with this problem and you are angry with me. Is there not a cause?" There is a reason. There is a cause. The situation has changed. The king is running. Captains are running. Brigades are running. Major Generals are running. Lieutenants are running. Lieutenant General, we do not know where his stars have fallen. The Sergeant Major is hiding in a cave. Is there not a cause? Is this not enough for you to say, "David, at least for thinking of the solution, you must be encouraged." Nobody wants to encourage him. You must recognize your moment of history when it comes.

It is the moment that God opens a door and when He opens, He is not going to open it wide. It is a small opening and when you see that door, you see, "This is my appointed time. I have the equipment. I have the training. I have the orientation. I have the mindset for this moment." Do not wait for the encouragement. Step into that opportunity because that is what is going to turn around your situation. The protocol may not allow you. Tradition may not allow you. Culture may not allow you. Your age may even disqualify you, but when it is your moment, it is your moment. Faith must recognize the moment in history.

Thirdly, **faith must value your past relevant achievements not irrelevant achievements, but** achievements you have made in the past that convinces you that you can take care of this problem. David said, "You know, I did not really make much of it. I did not think it was valuable but one day, a lion came against one of my sheep and it was running very fast. It was a moving target and I was away from it. I could not fight it physically, but I got my sling and I hold a stone and as fast as the lion was moving, sixty miles per hour, I knocked it down. It was faster, it was smaller, but I got it. This is bigger and he is slow and I can get it."

He says, "I remember another time a bear also came and I did the same. So I have solved problems of comparable nature even more difficult assignments, although nobody saw me solving them but I saw it. I was there. I did it in the secret place because it has prepared me for this public spectacle to value my past relevant achievements." God does not take you through what you have been through for nothing. He takes you through it so He can do something greater with your life.

You have to stay with your strengths. They tried to change David's arms. Saul tried to put the ammunition, his ammunition on David. That is a good effort. Saul is a nice man, but if the ammunition worked, why were you running away? I mean if it worked, why did not you go and deal with the giant yourself? The arms Saul had also had a spear. Its reach was forty feet. That is all. The man too had forty feet. Very soon you will be close and they knew they could not fight him so Saul knew his armors was useless, but he had never conceived that there was an alternate solution. When the nation is perplexed, the community is perplexed, the society is perplexed because they have fixed the solution, only one angle and they believe this is the only way to solve the problem. May God turn your eye to something else. May you find the answer that nobody has discovered yet. Stay with your strengths. David said to Saul, "I am not going to go with this. I have never used them before."

Trust in the name of the Lord. As prepared as you are, you have to go in the name of the Lord. Some trust in horses and chariots, but we trust in the name of the Lord. David was prepared but he said, "I come in the name of the Lord."

He did not say, "I come in the name of David, the son of Jesse." No. He was ready, but he came in the name of the Lord. Do not let your preparation substitute God's power. You are prepared, but trusting God. You are ready, but trust God. Believe God. Yield to him because there are unseen factors that only He can take off.

Lastly, the faith's response is **to boldly confront the challenge**. David confronted the challenge in **two ways:**

He spoke against it.

He ran towards it because every challenge has got a voice. Every Goliath has got a voice. You may not hear audibly but sometimes you hear it in your mind in your spirit, sometimes you hear it on the radio. It tells you, "You are good-for-nothing." It tells you, "You cannot do it." When you live in a country like Ghana, which has probably the most advanced qualification in criticism and complaining and murmuring, we have gone beyond PhD, we are now doing more sophisticated degrees like XYt not a PhD. We are doing deeper studies into memory, complaining, and criticism. "We cannot do it! We cannot do it!! We are suffering. It is not possible. It cannot be done. It has never been done." Some people will even say, "Even Kwesi Broni could not solve it." Once they say that, it means, "You, Kofi Bibini, how can you solve this? Akwesi himself could not do it. How can you solve it?"

When you live in this environment, you hear so much negativity and Goliath comes to David and says, "I will get you down. Am I a dog? I am going to knock you down and I will give your carcasses to the birds of the air." He is threatened, this young teenager, but David could not allow it to go. He also had to speak. When you hear negativity, you must speak positively. When you hear people tell you that you cannot do it, tell them, "I can do it. I can do all things through Christ in this nation. Not to suffer. I am here to be the head and not the tail." The problems that happen around you are designed to put fear into you and I am sure some of you, manufacturers, you have already said, "Ah, we are finished. We are dead. There is no electricity." But do you know, sometimes, when everybody says, "It cannot be done." There may be just one little door of opportunity and if you just stay positive with God, He will just open your eyes to see Goliath is not as powerful as he appears. You can still defeat him. Price tag is high. The value is high and God can give you the solution. Do not allow the depression around you to consume your spirit.

David had to learn to speak to the problem. I am sure David had been taught all his life to respect elders and not to speak back when elders speak. He saw this elder, saying, "He will eat him up." Normal culture would have said, "Oh, please, Sir, I am sorry, Sir. Please, Sir, I am a little boy. My meat is small. Do not destroy me." That is culture. At that time, David said, "Well, I have been told to respect elders, but this elder is defying the God I worship and I must rise tall and speak what God says out of my mouth."

He ran into the battle. The rest is history. Defeating Goliath will offer you four benefits. When you defeat Goliath, when everyone is running away from Goliath, these are the four recompenses you will receive. You will receive rewards for your effort (1 Samuel 17:25-26). David was told the rewards for defeating Goliath. He will get a good wife, which was good for him. He was told his family will be enriched. The King will enrich him and apart from that he will not pay taxes.

Anybody who makes money and does not pay taxes is a happy man, especially if he has a nice wife by his side. David was rewarded. Defeating Goliath brings you rewards for your effort.

Secondly, **it brings you recognition in high places** (1 Samuel 17:55-58). When Saul saw David, running after the armies of the Philistines, this young boy, he says, "Whose son is that?" The interesting thing is, David had been before Saul already. He had actually been playing music for Saul and casting out demons from him, but they were not big problems. Although he was before Saul, Saul never took note of him. Can you imagine? The guy sat in front of him, but he was nothing. He was just another musician in town who comes to play music for the king and the king had never registered the image of this boy in his mind.

When he sees what is happening, he begins to wonder who that boy is. Some of you have done some things in the past nobody recognized you for it. You achieved success and nobody gave you the credit, but God is bringing a Goliath your way and when you deal with that Goliath problem, people will begin to take recognition because the success you get when you overcome Goliath cannot be hidden. You get recognition in high places.

Thirdly, when you defeat Goliath, you get **the respect of the community** (1 Samuel 18:5-7). David, right after that, rose up in the army and he began to lead the army and the Bible says, "The people respected him because he behaved himself wisely." All the Captains of the army submitted to him. All of a sudden, this boy, who a few days ago, was just a shepherd boy, no military training is now leading the army and the people respected his command.

When God elevates you, even those who are older than you, more experienced than you, more educated than you, will begin to respect you because you will behave yourself wisely and nobody can fault you.

Finally, when you defeat Goliath, the forth blessing you receive is **resentment of the envious**. It is a blessing. There will be women who will sing your praise and there will be envious people who will "eye" you. I like how the Bible puts it, "... and Saul eyed David." It is almost as if he is a Ghanaian. He eyed him. He looked at him with evil eyes. David did not tell the women to sing. The women were singing their own song. He did not compose it for them, although he is a musician. He did not give them the lyrics. He did not create the poem. He was just a young boy who had won a victory and was just having fun and all of a sudden, the music of the town has changed. All the radio status are talking about David. The FM stations. "David, David, David. David, David, David."

The newspapers hit with the headlines, "David does it. All hail David. David the new king." The king looks at it and his eyes begin to change and he eyed him from that day onwards. It leads him to the next level in the process of becoming a king because many times, when you win victories and everybody praises you and you have no enemy, it gets into your head. So God will give you an eyeing Saul to keep you on the right track. Can you imagine if everybody had praised David and the king is praising him, his father is praising him, this boy will self-destruct. He will think, "I have arrived. Hey, look at me. I am the new boss and everybody likes me." He will go to excesses and excesses and destroy himself. So God will give you a remnant who is not moved by your success. A remnant God appointed to eye you.

You hear them say, "They hate me. They are the Devil. The Devil is a liar." It is not the Devil; it is God who leaves them to help you not to destroy yourself. They will help you to keep your perspective right. They help you to be on the alert every time, so you do not lose guard and allow your enemy to destroy you. Those who eye you, keep you on track. When you know people are envious of you and want to destroy you, you do not want to give them the pleasure of watching over your distraction. Sometimes because of them you do not mess up. You say to yourself, "I am not going to do it for that man to laugh and say, 'Erh, we said it! We said it!!" "I will not give him that pleasure." That is the role of an eyeing, the envious man, anointed with eye and anointed to envy.

When they start on your track, you will pray continuously, they do not change. These people do not change, nor repeat nor reform. They are the same yesterday, today and forever. They will envy you till the end. You will find out as we study more. You will find out Saul never changed. People came to talk to him, he never changed. People tried to change his mind, he never changed. When David saved his life, he never changed. He himself vowed to David, "David, I am a bad man. I have offended you. Forgive me please. From now onwards, I am a bad man."

He never changed. It is his job. If you expect an envious person to be your friend one day, you are Alice in Wonderland. You are out of reality. That person is in your life to keep you alert for the rest of your life so your success does not become your enemy. You are going to find people who resent you. I am sure there are people who do not like me. There are people who are eyeing me. "You, this boy, one day, you will see. We have left you to the wind." That is part of the job.

That is why David understood the value of Saul in his life. He never hated Saul. Do not ever hate those who resent you otherwise they will make you become like them. Do not envy them back. Do not hate them. Do not fight them. Do not criticize them. Do not try to destroy them. Leave them to play their role.

If God's Hand is upon you, they can never kill you. They can never destroy you. They can never stop you. They are just there to remind you that you have constantly trusted God every day of your life. That is their role. That is all they are doing. To keep you dependent on God, but as for the assignment they cannot stop you from getting there. Amen!

CHAPTER THREE – IN THE PALACE

This is going to be probably the pivotal piece in this manuscript. If you do not get anything at all, you have to get what this chapter is about. It is crucial to where God is taking you. As God elevates you, as He seeks to elevate you, He is taking you through a process and that process is leading you to the elevated place.

Part of the process is to bring you into the palace and I want to encourage you to let your heart grab and grasp this because in my experience this is where many people falter on their path to the throne. They falter in the palace.

1 Samuel 17:57-59, 18:1-5 is a continuous piece broken by Chapter 18 so it will be read as if, the Chapter does not exist. There will be no pause at verse 58; just a continuation to Chapter 18 and start from verse 1. This cause and situation occurred after David had conquered Goliath. Let us start with the reading of God's Word.

"Then, as David returned from the slaughter of the Philistine, Abnor took him and brought him before Saul with the head of the Philistine in his hand. And Saul said to him, 'Whose son are you, young man?' Then David answered, 'I am the son of your servant, Jesse, the Bethlehemite.'

"Now when he had finished speaking to Saul, the soul of Jonathan was knit to the soul of David and Jonathan loved him as

his own soul. Saul took him that day and would not let him go home to his father's house anymore.

"Then Jonathan and David made a covenant because he loved him as his own soul and Jonathan took off the robe that was on him and gave it to David with his armor even his sword and his bow and his belt. So David went out wherever Saul sent him and behaved wisely and Saul set him over the men of war and he was accepted in the sight of all people and also in the sight of Saul's servant."

After David had won this great victory, Saul takes this young boy who has accomplished such a magnificent work for the whole nation and told him from this day you are not going to go to your home any longer. So he took him out of the house of Jesse and brought him to the palace of Saul.

The palace represents **the environment of favor, power and opportunity. It is the place where things happen.** God allows Saul to take David from his father's house to a place of importance and the place of opportunity and the place of power and the place of favor. When you enter the palace, you are going to experience all these things; you are going to experience favor, you are going to see opportunity and that is why being in the palace is crucial to getting to the throne. The path to the palace is powered by **three activities: three different things will bring you to the palace.**

The first to bring you to the palace is **God's grace**. When God looks at you and shows you favor and His grace, and it is the grace of God that separated David from his brothers and anointed him in the midst of his brothers. There were more qualified people, more experienced people, better equipped people, people with better stature and better military training but they were all bypassed. David could be selected. That is God's grace.

The second thing that brings you to the palace is **your own personal achievement.** David got to the palace not through bribery and corruption; not through favoritism, but because he proved by his own accomplishment that he was worthy of acceptance. His own personal achievement brought him to the palace.

The third thing that brings you to the palace is **the King's recognition.** You can work as hard as you want. Be as good as you are but if the king does not spot you and you do not catch the eye of the king, you will remain a hardworking person with no favor, no power, no opportunity but somehow David caught the king's eye.

If you go to Ghana's parliament, you will get to know that a parliamentarian has to be able to do is to catch the speaker's eye. If you have a statement to make, ten people may raise up their hands, but somebody must catch the speaker's eye. For him to be singled out. So it is not how high you raise your hand or how much information you have but the man must notice you.

In David's case, he was noticed by the king and he was brought into the palace firstly because of God's grace upon his life, secondly because of his own personal achievement, thirdly because of the recognition of the king. The recognition of the king is the icing on the cake. I want you to note that the palace is not the throne. It prepares you for the throne. When you get to the palace, you have not arrived. It is only a preparation. You are brought to the place of favor, to the place of power, to the place of opportunity. You are in the corridors of power, but it is not the power. It is not the throne. It is preparation. It is so important to get this because many people are brought to the palace and when they get there, they feel they have arrived and they make terrible mistakes in the palace and never get to the throne.

In my lifetime, I have seen people with great potential, people who have achieved much, people who have been recognized brought to the palace and in the palace, they assumed they were on the throne and because they assumed they were on the throne, they behaved not like people in the palace but people on the throne.

Remember in the palace, there is only one throne and the king is the one who sits on it. Everybody else is a servant. You may be excellent servant, most high servant, supreme servant but a servant. I want you to get that. You may be called servant of whatever, but you are a servant. It is like in government, there is only one President. Everybody is a minister. Minister means servant. So you may be Minister of Health, you are a servant for health, Minister of Education – servant for education, Minister of Defense – servant for defense, for whatever. If you do not have the understanding that there is only one king and everybody else is a servant, you are going to get yourself into a lot of hot water.

It is not only in government. It is in corporate organizations. It is in industry. It is in the church. It is in relationships at home, but if you come to the palace, you do not understand the difference between the throne and activities in the palace, you are going to make such a long rope that will hang your own self. This is where a lot of people fail to arrive at the throne. So what was David's role in the palace? What was he supposed to do? There are three important things I am going to talk about that David did in the palace. I believe, if you want God to elevate you, in this season and year of elevation as God promotes people, you need to know how to position yourself otherwise there will be a promotion of your life, but you may never get there not because God failed you but because your attitude undermined the grace of God upon your life.

The first thing you have to learn to do, the first thing David learnt to do, is **how to please the king**. That was the lesson David learnt. David understood that he was in the place because he killed Goliath, but what if the king had not recognized that he killed Goliath, he will still be running after sheep. So he understood, "Yes, I am anointed. God's grace is upon me. Yes, I killed Goliath, but I am here because this man brought me here. He brought me into the palace. He introduced me to this opportunity, to this power. He exposed me to these trappings of power and David understood that his number one job in the palace was to please the king and so he Bible says, "He went wherever the king sent him and he discharged his duties well."

Wherever the king went, he went too. He did not complain, "Well, I do not feel like going there. I do not feel this is what I should do. After killing Goliath, I do not think this is my job." Interestingly, when you read the first job that David had after killing Goliath was the previous job he had before he killed Goliath. Before killing Goliath, he sat with a harp and played when the king was moody and depressed. He did not mind because nobody knew him. He will play and sing about, "The Lord being his shepherd and the Lord surrounds us. As the mountain surrounds Jerusalem, so the Lord surrounds us." And as he sang those songs and began to worship, praise God, the spirit of depression will leave Saul and he will begin to dance and glorify God and go to bed peacefully.

At that time, Saul never asked who that boy was, who played music for him. He did not care. All he wanted was music. Then David killed Goliath and you will think, Saul will say, "Well, from now onwards, you will stop doing what you used to do." He brings him back to play his music. This time, he is playing music after great achievement. If you do not know you are there to please the king, after you kill Goliath, you will not go back to play the music you used to play because you will think you have graduated from there. David understood, "I am not here to serve myself. I am here to serve the king. If the king wants music, I will give him music, although I think I can do more than that, this is what he wants. That is what I give him." That is all. So he continues to play the music.

At this time, it was more dangerous that the first because the king was eyeing him. You know how difficult it is to please somebody who is eyeing you? **So how do you please the king?**

Firstly, **bury your personal agenda**. Many people go to the palace with their own agenda. They believe they are supposed to be on the throne. They believed they are supposed to be the head. They walk with a spring in their steps and a chip on their shoulders. They feel big for their ten little tons and they walk with a sense of importance. "I have arrived." They have their own agenda. They start printing their own complimentary cards. "David, son of Jesse, killer of Goliath."

When the king has a visitor, they say, "Well, can you just have my card? You can give me a call." Personal agenda in the palace will take you back to the sheepfold. You do not go to the palace to serve your own personal agenda. You have to learn to kill your agenda. Yes, you believe God has great plans for you. Whilst you are there serving, forget that God said, "You will be king" and just serve for the moment otherwise you will have a conflict of interest – your own interest and the interest of the king whose palace you have come into. Bury your personal achievement.

Secondly, **genuinely seek the king's interest** not hypocrisy. You go to the king and say, "Sire, what are you doing this morning? I hope you are feeling fine. I heard that something happened and I just wanted to come and encourage you, 'It shall be well.' " Many people work for people but never seek the interest of the people they work for. They like his salary, but never seek his interests. How many of you in your companies have ever remembered to give your boss a card on his birthday. "Well, I am not here to please man." That is one of the most annoying statements. You are not here to please man. Who signed your letter of appointment? Was it not man? There are people who say, "It is not man who brought me here. It is God who brought me here." Did God give you the appointment? When you went for the interview, was it God who interviewed you? It was a man. If you do not learn to honor and respect the man who sits in front of you, how can you honor God whom you do not see? You have to genuinely seek his interest. When his enemies become your enemies, his friends become your friends when he is being fought, you fight those who fight him.

When he is criticized, you stand against those critics. People will know that they cannot play games with you and that man. That is genuinely seeking the interest of the king in the palace. Not advancing your agenda which is very easy for most people to do.

The third thing in pleasing the king is **to stay away from aggrieved servants**. Every palace has got aggrieved servants, frustrated, bitter, long service, and unfulfilled servants. People who feel something has gone wrong with them and anytime you come into the palace, they enlist you into their army and infect you with their grievances. Grievances the person has not experienced, he is made to accept as if he has also experienced it. They do not tell them about the mistakes they did to be treated the way they have been treated. They only talk about the wrong that has been done to them.

Some of you, unfortunately, go to places of power and influence and you allow aggrieved servants to recruit you and you forget you are there because the king recognized you and decided to bring you to this palace to give you exposure. If you do not understand that, you will kill yourself before your day of promotion. Stay away from bitterness, disloyal troops, people who have served for a long time and now are becoming very critical. They poison the atmosphere. Go to every office. They are there. Most of the time, they are the longest serving people. They are there and they are bitter and every word of their mouth is poisoned.

Unfortunately, some of you have become that in your offices, in your companies. That is how you behave and you wonder how you are now getting to the throne. Who will promote a saboteur, a subversive rebel? Who will do that? Nobody in his right mind will do that.

To please the king, you have to perform your tasks faithfully. Wherever David was sent, the Bible says, "He would go." Sometimes he went to dangerous places. The king sent him on dangerous missions and he would go. Personal assignments he would go. Protocol assignments he would go. "Go and meet that king and give him a message." "Go and meet that General and send him a message." "Go and do that" and he will go. Now how difficult was it for David? It was difficult for David because at this time all the FM stations were playing the latest record in town, "Saul has killed his thousands and David has killed his ten thousands." It was on every FM station. It was in every newspaper, people had it on their Walkman, CD player, iPods and everybody was singing, "Saul, thousand; David, ten thousand…"

Now if you hear that song in your ear, you begin to think, "You have arrived. All the people like me. I am popular. Everybody wants me." You forget you are in the palace because the king recognized you and called you to the palace. If you do not understand that simple principle, you will hurt yourself. Many people are frustrated in life because where they think they must be they have not gotten there and this is one of the cardinal reasons. They went to the palace to pursue their agenda and their self-interest and they wallow at the same level. They go in circles, never upwards.

The second thing David did and which you must do when you enter the palace is that you must learn to observe protocol. David understood protocol. He understood where he had come from and he understood the moods of the king. Unfortunately, David was under a very moody, depressed, melancholic person who vacillates from one end to the other. One moment he is happy, "Alleluia! Hey!" Next moment, he is moody. Nobody wants to go to his office. That is King Saul and David had to learn to manage that conflict in his leader. He understood and observed a protocol. How do you observe protocol in the king's palace?

Protect privileged information. By virtue of the fact that you are in the palace and in the presence of the king, you will be exposed to information that other people are not exposed to. So David was there, he saw that the king was demon possessed. The rest of the population thought he was a great king. David saw how the man behaved when demons entered him. He saw the weakness of the man – the humanity of the man. If David was not matured, he will go all around and say, "You, people, you do not know. The person you call king, he is demon possessed. I am telling you. I am there in the palace myself. I sit before him and the things he does, I cannot tell you."

Many people think that gossiping about privileged information is a sign of importance and power, but it is a sign of weakness, betrayal and unfaithfulness. If you work with a king, with a leader, with a boss in his office and you are exposed to information people do not normally have, you have to keep your mouth shut because by virtue of proximity to power, everything you see, everything you hear is privileged and you do not use the name of the king to advance your personal agenda. Those who go around saying, "Well, the king said, 'I should do this.' "

They never take initiative, even when the king has instructed you, you take his instruction, and you make it your personal responsibility. So when it fails, people will not say the king did it, they will say you did it and they will kill you and keep the king alive. That is why when there is a kingdom, the refrain of the king is, "God saved the king." He is more important than every subject. It is better he is protected than for other people to protect themselves.

For people to go and say, "Well, you know we were at the meeting and some of us did not agree with what was happening but what can we do? The man is the boss so sometimes he gets crazy and he says it." You are a joker in the palace. You have no idea what leadership is all about. Protect privileged information.

Secondly, learn to behave wisely. When you go to the palace, you will get to know that the protocol around sheep is different from the protocol around kings. When you are around sheep, sheep do not care what you do. You can talk anyhow, eat anyhow, sit anyhow, dance anyhow, but when you go to the palace where diplomats come and other kings come to visit, you cannot be there walking, shouting, "Chale, how is it? Chale long time no see" and the king of Egypt has just visited the king or you see the king of Egypt coming and you say, "Eh, chale, what is going on, king?" You have to learn to behave yourself wisely. Talk wisely. Eat wisely.

Dress wisely. You cannot dress to the palace as you do to a football game. You have to understand the dress code – the protocol code. The language structure. Diplomatic language. You cannot just be talking by heart. The diplomats are there and you say, "As for me, I do not care. What I feel is what I say." It is just a sign of immaturity. Only children do what they feel like doing because they have no sense of discipline.

When you get disciplined, you do not do what you feel like doing; you do what is appropriate to be done. You cannot just talk anyhow. "Well, that is how I am. Leave it or take it." Then get out of the palace. You have to learn to talk with measured decorum. You even want to tell somebody is not intelligent and say, "Well, Sir, I think that the concept you have propounded are clearly your opinion, but they are not exactly adequate for the matter under discussion." Somebody asks, "What did he say?" The one who has ears will say, "He just insulted him, but he did it nicely."

You do not look at somebody in the palace and say, "You are a fool! You are a fool!!" How can you talk that way? Sometimes when I hear people who are in the corridors of power, talk like street people, I wonder what they are doing in the corridors of power because you must learn to behave yourself wisely so that nobody looks at your behavior and insults your king. Wise behavior.

Stay within your ranks and within your mandate. David knew where he had come from and where he was going. One of the things that endears David was that constantly in his lifetime, he never lost sight of his humble beginnings and when David was told, when he was going to fight Goliath, he was promised the king's daughter but he did not go to claim her afterwards. "I have killed the giant. Where is your daughter?" He just kept his distance. So the king came to him, "David, the girl is yours." David says, "Sir, you have no idea where I am coming from. In my family, we do not marry people like that. I am happy that you want to give me this, but I do not think I deserve her."

Then Saul went to tell David's friends, "Go and tell David. I want to give him my daughter." David says to his friends, "You people, do you know what you are talking about? This is the king's daughter. Do not talk about the king's daughter as if it is ordinary marriage. You know where I am coming from? In my family, nobody has married like that before."

He had to be persuaded to take that offer. People who do not understand protocol in the palace, even when you have not promised, they want to take and when you give it to them, they take it with your hand and pull you also. David understands the protocol. He understood his ranks. He understood his mandate. He understood his authority – how far he could go and how far he could not go. One of the most important things you must learn when you are in the palace is to know where your mandate ends because the king has authority you do not have. If for example in the political sphere, the President addresses the people and says, "My fellow Ghanaians, Good evening." When you are a Minister of state, you do not also make that address and say, "My fellow Ghanaians. Good evening." Whose fellow Ghanaians? You are just a servant with a title. When did you start addressing fellow Ghanaians?

You have to understand your mandate, your rank and do not imitate the things you do not have the power to do. Not everything of the king must be imitated because some of them, he makes them, due to the power he has. You do not have the power and if you mess up, you are in big trouble. Sometimes you see the king doing something, but when you are given the chance, you do not do it.

It is like church. A pastor can come to church and say, "Everybody, get up." People get up, laughing and nobody gets offended. The pastor founded the church. It is true. He even gave the name to the church. Can you imagine a young boy who does not have that authority, comes to say, "Everybody, get up." People will begin to say, "Who does he think he is?" If that person wants people to rise up, he will say, "Kindly rise up." It is different levels of authority. You have to know where your mandate ends otherwise you will create enemies, resentment. People are going to be annoyed. People are going to fight you. People are going to criticize you. People are going to rebel against you and ask you, "Who do you think you are?"

You have to understand your mandate and do not claim things that are done for the king as due you because they are not due you. That is why nobody has a say when the

President is being driven by his motorcade. It is annoying, is it not? And we the citizens are sitting in our cars and we are in traffic. He has gone. That is why he is the President. If you want a motorcade, stand for an election and win.

Avoid greed and opportunism. In the palace, you have to avoid greed and opportunism. It relates to staying within your ranks. Greed. Grabbing! Grabbing!! Grabbing!!! Opportunism. Every little thing, you want to take advantage of it. You go to the king's friends and you want to take something from them. If you want to live long in the palace and finally end up on the throne, when you are going to talk to the king's friends, seek permission from the king first. If one of them asks you for a favor, ask the king, "Your friend came to me and said, 'Do this.' Do you want me to do it?" If he says no, you do not do it.

If you want to go to a new palace, then resign from this palace and go to another palace but so far as you are here, that is how it is whether he is a king or she is a queen. Sometimes kings are queens. That is a woman. It happens. Your boss at the hairdressing salon, at the seamstress' place, your madam has customers and one of them comes to you and say, "Do something for me." And you do not go and ask the madam but you go behind and take the job. That is lack of palace protocol.

If somebody comes and says, "I want you to do this." You talk to your boss and say, "Listen. Mr. X wants me to do this. Is it ok with you? Do you think I should do it?" If he says, "Go" you go. If he says, "Do not go" you do not go even if the price is right and the money on it is loaded. You say, "Mm mm... this is my day of opportunity." You are not in the palace to pursue your agenda. You are there to please the king, to observe protocol.

Thirdly, **David was in the palace to mature in statecraft**. I was going to use leadership, but I chose the word state craft because state craft is not just leadership. It is the ability to wisely manage your own life within the content or context of power. It goes into the way you talk, the way you behave yourself and everything. It is state craft. You must mature in that. David had to mature in statecraft. He had to learn to advance between the faithful service to the king and the ability to keep himself from trouble.

Remember David was under the tutorship of one of the most impossible leaders. It is like being a Minister in the government of Field Marshall Idi Ami. That is how it is. That is how Saul was. He had such character and that is what David was serving. He was not serving under a nice person. He was suffering under a very difficult boss and whiles he was nice, playing his music and winning battles for the king; the king wanted to kill him. State craft then comes in. You do not say, "Well, let me protect this and be loyal; be totally ignorant of conspiracies around me."

David knew how to balance both very well. That is state craft. He knew how to stay on both sides of the king. His good side and his bad side. How do you mature in statecraft? You start spiritually. You have to grow in grace and spiritual understanding. If you do not grow spiritually, if you do not get in deep spiritually, you will handle a lot of things in the flesh. People fight you in the flesh, you fight back in the flesh, so you have to grow in grace and spiritual understanding. Grow in the spirit. Mature in the spirit because a lot of battles you have to fight, they may appear like human beings fighting you, but they are also spiritual battles and you have to learn to organize yourself well.

What I like about David is that in this context, he grew closer to the Lord. He found favor with God. He grew into the things of the Spirit and so he could understand the spiritual dynamics of what was happening in his life. Instead of just looking at it physically and trying to kill Saul back. So you have to grow in grace and spiritual understanding.

Secondly, **you have to study and understand human nature**. Human nature is a very, very, very complicated system. Somebody can love you and destroy you at the same time. Human nature can do things unpredictably. Somebody loves his wife so much so that he beats her and then cries afterwards. Recently, a wife poured acid on her husband for buying her enough food to eat. It is the complication of the human nature. People do silly things with good intentions. People do criminal things with good intentions and so you have to understand human nature that sometimes, somebody may smile but his nature is different. He says, "Come closer. Come closer. Come closer" and he wants to stab you so you have to understand human nature.

The man says, "You know I love you. You are the best." Whiles he is saying that, he has told other people to destroy you. So you have to understand. You have to be smart. David understood that and I believe every time he was in the presence of Saul, he was on high alert because Saul will take a spear and throw it at David and he will dodge. If he was not alert, he could not dodge. The man was on high alert. Every muscle was tensed up and he was playing the harp; his eyes are going this way and that way, "The Lord is my shepherd" and he is going out there. He was smart in that and he never took the spear back to fight Saul, but he made sure he would not be destroyed before his time. You have to understand human nature that people can be very unpredictable. They can act in very, very bad ways sometimes. That is why, sometimes, God will take you out of the palace, which we will find in the next stage of David becoming a king.

Gain the trust of your colleagues. That is what happened to David. He gained the trust of the Jonathan. He did not conspire with Jonathan against Saul, but that relationship with Jonathan, who was the number two person in the kingdom protected David many times and Jonathan trusted him like his soul according to the Scriptures. Can you imagine your boss' son trusts you and your boss wants to kill you? It is a very difficult balance.

Jonathan was a very interesting character. He never criticized his father, never fought his father, but he also knew, sometimes, his father's dictates were murderous. And so he played between pleasing his father and also protecting his best friend. He did it so well. In the end, he died for doing that, but he was a very astute diplomat. So in the palace, gain the trust of your colleagues. There must be people who trust you, believe in you, who will watch for your interest even when trouble is looming. They will not conspire with you, to fight the king, destroy the king and take the throne by force, but they can alert you to say, "Listen. I think you should not be saying those things. You have been saying because the king is not happy with that statement. That press conference you had, I think, you should tone it down because the king is not happy. That interview with Joy FM is not helping your case."

There must be a Jonathan who is able to whisper words of guidance to you, but if you are just walking around, "I believe I am protected." One day, something will hit you. "What hit me?" So you need to gain the trust of your colleagues.

Finally, to mature in statecraft, **you have to accept challenging assignments**. David saw every assignment as a means for him to grow as a statesman even assignments that had dubious intentions. Like what Saul told him to do in order to have his daughter as a wife. The wife has already been promised for the head of Goliath. He deserved it. Then Saul gave him another assignment which I do not want to go into details on but you can read it for yourself. You realize the reason Saul gave him that assignment was because he felt that this time David was going to die but David took it up and he fought. He took challenging assignments. He did not say, "Well, the man wants me to do this to destroy me so I will not do it." He just trusted God with the assignment. He did it well and the Bible says, "David behaved himself wisely and Saul feared him the more." He matured. He did not shirk from responsibility. He took his challenge wisely.

In the palace, you have to watch out for what I call bad palace language. Remember your attitude and language in the palace is crucial to your promotion on the throne. That means you have to avoid some attitudes and some words.

The first thing you have to avoid in the palace is **pride**. Anything that says, "I am better than the boss. The people are even saying it. All the people say it. Things are working because of me. If it was not me, he will suffer. I am better." That is pride. Watch that language in the palace that you see yourself better than the king.

Secondly, **the language of criticism**. "This place is bogus. This place is bad. Nothing happens here. Everything here is bad. Look at that. Look at how he is walking. Look at his legs. Just avoid it. Let someone else do it." Do not be lazy. In the palace, you do not say, "Let someone else do it." When you are given the job, you take it and you do it. Do not be lazy. Take advantage on the tasks, the responsibilities that you have.

Anger. Be careful of anger. "This place will burn. Hmm…" Sometimes you find workers who say, "We will destroy the place." The place that has given you employment, given your salary to pay your children's school fees. If you are leaving, leave quietly so that someone will come and get his salary and pay his children's school fees, but you want to leave and you want to destroy it before you leave. It was there before you came. When you leave, it should be there. Do not burn it down. Do not destroy it because if you do not need it, someone else may need it.

Do you know, sometimes you can complain about salary and say, "Oh, I do not like the salary here. We are leaving." Someone else will come and take the job because if you do not like it, someone does. You say, "The pay is too low." It may be low for you. It may be hell for you. It may be heaven for somebody so if you do not like it, quietly leave. Do not burn it down. Leave for somebody else to benefit from it.

Maybe you have grown beyond it. Your skills are beyond it. Your expectations are beyond it. Go somewhere else where your skills will be dependent. Leave that place for somebody else to come and find help just like you found help when you came the first time. "This was the best place in the world." If you have outgrown it, leave, but let somebody else benefit. Do not burn the place up.

Greed. The language that says, "I deserve more than I get." No matter how well you try to help, the language of greed is always never satisfied. It is not a genuine desire. It is greed. "I want more because he has more. Look at him. He is sitting down there with his big head and he is drinking tea in his air condition office and we are here suffering." That is why you are not the Managing Director and when you become Managing Director, switch off the air conditioner and do not drink the tea, donate the money to the company. It does not work that way. It is only greed that says, "I deserve more than I can get."

Remember this that the palace is not the throne. It only prepares you for the throne. When God brings you to the palace, you have not arrived. It is not the throne. Do not throw your weight about. It is only preparing you for your future.

CHAPTER FOUR – WILDERNESS LIFE

God chose David. David faced Goliath and he was recognized and brought into the palace. Now he is at the fourth phase of his life – in the wilderness. Each one of us, on the journey to the throne, will go through a period of wilderness training. Every great leader has a wilderness experience. Moses had one before he was called to go and liberate Israel from Egypt. John the Baptist, the Bible says, was in the wilderness until the day of his manifestation. Jesus Christ, after He had had an open Heaven encounter as soon as he was baptized, was driven by the spirit to the wilderness to be tempted before he began His Ministry.

Wherever God wants to take you, He will also take you through the wilderness. In the life of David, he had several wilderness experiences. As a matter of fact, David had three wilderness experiences.

The first one was before he was even recognized by God. He was in the wilderness, taking care of the sheep.

Then after he was recognized, he went to the palace and to the wilderness.

And then after he got to the throne, his son Absalom, rebelled against him and he went into the wilderness. That simply tells you that it is not going to come once in your lifetime. You will have a few of those wilderness experiences.

"And David stayed in the strongholds in the wilderness and remained in the mountains of the wilderness of Ziph but God did not deliver him into His Hand. So David saw that Saul had come out to seek his life and David was in the wilderness of Ziph in a forest." (1 Samuel 23:14-15) Here two verses are captured that express the condition of David at this phase in his life as he is seeking to become the person has called him to be.

Three times in these two verses, we are introduced to the location of David that he is in a wilderness and in the strongholds of the wilderness. The strongholds were the caves, the protected spaces in the wilderness. So what happens when you are in the wilderness? There are four things that happen when you are in the wilderness.

The wilderness, first of all, is a place of wondering. A place where you keep moving without settling. You keep going continuously and changing. There is uncertainty. You do not stay. You are not permanent and there is no sense of permanency in your life. It is a wilderness experience. You put your hand to do something, it does not work. You put your hand to another thing, it does not work and you keep moving and moving and moving. The wilderness experience is a wondering experience.

Secondly, **the wilderness is a place of tests and trials**. In the wilderness, you go through difficulties, challenges and sometimes they come from every side. Jesus, in His wilderness was tested, tempted. The wilderness experience is a time of testing and trials.

Thirdly, it is not just a time of testing and trials, but also **it is a time of strengthening.** That is the time you build your strength. So it is not altogether a negative experience, it is also a time of strengthening. You have time to reflect, to be instructed and then you build or rebuild your strengths.

Fourthly, **the wilderness experience is designed to be an experience of transformation.** In the wilderness, we experience God's power of transformation to be the kind of person he wants us to be. It was said of Jesus before He entered the wilderness, the Bible says, "He was full of the Spirit." After His temptation, the Bible says, "He came in the power of the Spirit." Transformation where what you are full of, becomes practical, applicable power in your life.

Each one of us, at every stage in our lives, will go through a wilderness experience. I can guarantee some of you are in a wilderness experience right now. Some of you are coming out and some of you are entering. Life in the wilderness is caused by **two factors**. Two factors will drive you into the wilderness.

Wilderness experience can be **seen driven**. When your sins take you into the wilderness. That is, when you make wrong choices and you suffer the consequences. When you are in the wilderness because of sin and wrong choices, you are required to repent.

Secondly, life in the wilderness can be **spiritually driven.** When it is spirit driven, it is God's divine agenda and His purpose and it requires obedience. The Israelites had a wilderness experience not because they were driven by the spirit, but because of their disobedience, their wrong choices and their sins. They spent forty years in the wilderness. Jesus also went to the wilderness, the Bible says, "He was driven by the Spirit." So there are two forces that can take you into the wilderness – your own mistakes or the spirit. If it is your own mistake, the only way to come out of the wilderness is to repent. If it is the Spirit of God leading you, the way to come out of the wilderness is to obey God.

Many of us are in wilderness experiences not because God took us there, but because we took ourselves there by our own bad choices. David went into the wilderness. It was not his choice. It was not because it was sin driven, but it was part of God's agenda for him to go there. It was spirit driven. In the wilderness, there are **three things** I am going to talk about the experiences of David in the wilderness and I believe that they are experiencing some of us can identify with and are familiar with because they are experiences we all go through.

The first experience of David in the wilderness was **personal loneliness**. As a matter of fact, you have to understand that the way to the top is a lonely road. The top is so narrow that you do not have companions up there – at the top. Companions are at the bottom. It is like a pyramid. The higher you go, the narrower it becomes and in life, you will realize that the higher you go, the more friends you lose. The lower you are, the more friends you have because there are many who are like you at the bottom, but as you go up, you find only a few people who think like you, who believe like you and who aspire to what you are aspiring for.

You find only a few people who are like minded, even the people around you may not be like-minded so in that sense, you may have a crowd around you and still be very lonely because you do not have like-minded people. When I read 1 Samuel 21:1, it struck me so deeply. This is after David had run away from Saul, and Saul continues to eye David. He is very unsure of him and makes a lot of effort to kill David. David avoids it. Jonathan, Saul's son, tries to intervene and his father almost kills him for trying to protect David. So now Jonathan is convinced, "His father wants to kill David." He makes an arrangement with David and finally gives a queue for David to run away into the wilderness.

When David ran into the wilderness, the stop he comes to is this verse, 1 Samuel 21:1, and something just struck my spirit.

"Now David came to Nob, to Ahimelech, the priest and Ahimelech was afraid when he met David and said to him, "Why are you alone and no one is with you?" (1 Samuel 21:1).

Here is a man who has had people around him. The women are singing his praises. His name is in the news and everybody is praising him. He is popular. He is famous and all of a sudden nobody is with him. His life is in his hands and he is running alone. Sometimes in life, you will find popular, great people, people who are in the news, and then you meet them one day somewhere and they are alone. There is nobody there and they are left to themselves to fight their own battles. Those who said, "Saul has killed his thousands, David, his ten thousands" have turned off the radio and they have gone back looking for the next hero to sing his praises and now you are alone.

The wilderness experience is a time of personal loneliness. When all the people who used to support you for one reason or the other leave, some for fear of their lives and if you read that account, Ahimelech, the priest himself, was afraid because everybody knew David was under the microscope of Saul.

If you identify with David, you are in big trouble and if you do not know anything about this world, when you are in trouble, you lose friends very fast because people want to associate with success but not with trouble when you are on top, everybody likes you. You attract sycophants, hypocrites, and "parasites" in large numbers, but when you do not have the trappings of power, they all leave you. Under personal loneliness, what happened to David? He was stripped of all royal privileges. Here is a man who, a few weeks ago, was eating at the king's palace.

He was royalty, the king's son-in-law. The General in the army. The defeater of Goliath. His family was tax-free. He had rights, privileges, opportunities, doors were opened for him and now he is stripped of all royal privileges and you will get to know when you are stripped of all royal privileges, you lose friends very fast. Those who come to you because you give them money will come no more because you have no money. Those who need you to open a door for them will come to you no more because you cannot open your own door. All the favors are gone.

Ask politicians. It is just unfortunate that in Ghana politicians do not write their memoirs, but I think all politicians should write their memoirs – their story especially those who move from office. Stripped of everything and all of a sudden you are alone and that was what happened to David. Alone. He is no longer a royal person. He is just a fugitive on the run.

Not only is he stripped of all royal privileges, he is surrounded by powerful enemies. Everywhere he goes, there are spies of Saul around to send information back to Saul and if you read further down this story, when he went to Ahimelech, to ask for food and for military arms for him to protect himself, in that place, there was a man who had come to worship God to wait before God but the man was a servant of Saul who saw David and quickly the information is sent to Saul. When you are in this situation, you have nowhere to hide because you are surrounded on every side by people who are seeking your downfall.

Thirdly, **David is seized by fear and suspicion**. When people are in the wilderness and they are alone and abandoned, fear grips them and they begin to be very suspicious of everybody. They do not know whom to trust because they have been betrayed by trusted people and David went through that situation. He did not know whom to trust. Who is my friend? Who is for me? Who is against me? Who will speak for me?

In that situation, his main desire was to find a hiding place. He was seeking for a hiding place. The wilderness experience is a very lonely experience. If you are there right now, do not be discouraged. David was also there. Jesus was also there. Moses was also there. Paul the apostle was also there. Every significant leader was there some time ago. You will come out. It is not a permanent state of life. It is a transition to your destiny. Maybe your sin took you there; all you need to do is to repent and ask God to forgive you and change your choices and move out of the wilderness, but if it is the Holy Spirit who has driven you there, do not be afraid at all. Just obey God one step at a time. Today there is nobody singing your praise, but they are going to come back. The story will change because a wilderness experience is not a permanent experience. It is transitory and it has an end. It is part of your training. It is part of the building of your character.

What happens is the lonelier you are, the more dependent on God you are. When Jesus had no food to eat, the only food He could eat was the Word of God. So when He was tempted, He said, "Man shall not live by bread alone, but by every Word that comes out of the mouth of God." He had learned to stop depending on natural sustenance and start depending on spiritual sustenance.

In your wilderness experience, when you feel lonely, embrace God. Is it not amazing that sometimes when powerful people go through a wilderness experience, they become open to God? They start serving God. When a very prominent person goes to prison, they start reading their Bible and people say, "It is hypocrisy." It is not hypocrisy. It is that when all men abandon you and you have only one source to go to and that is Jehovah and He never abandons you. When people come to the end of themselves, they know that beyond the end of themselves there is a way and it is the way of God. They are not being hypocrites. They have just found the way out of the wilderness. It is to cultivate a relationship with God. The wilderness is a time of personal loneliness. If you are there, you will come out.

Secondly, **the wilderness experience is a time of public humiliation**. The loneliness is personal, you are the only one who feels it, but the humiliation, and everyone is going to see it. The wilderness experience, most of the time, will bring with it public humiliation. Many of us have gone through that before.

1 Samuel 21:10-15 is an account that breaks my heart. As I read it, I can just feel what is going on in the life of this young man. He is sitting somewhere. He has not said he wants to be king. On the day Samuel comes, he calls him out. He anoints him and then one day he goes, he sees Goliath. He tries a trick on Goliath. He throws a stone. Goliath is down. The king promises him everything and he

believes this is a sweet life. Then the king gets upset with him and everything is now against him.

"Then David arose and fled that day from before Saul and went to Achish, the king of Gath, and the servants of Achish said to him, 'Is this not David, the king of the land? Did they not sing to him to one another in dances, saying, 'Saul has slain his thousands, and David his ten thousands.' Now David took these words to heart and was very much afraid of Achish, the king of Gath. So he changed his behavior before them, pretended madness in their hands, scratched on the doors of the gate, and let his saliva fall down on his beard.

"Then Achish said to his servants, 'Look. You see the man is insane. Why have you brought him to me? Have I need of madmen that you have brought this fellow to play the madman in my presence? Shall this fellow come into my house?' " (1 Samuel 21:10-15).

Here is the anointed king behaving in the most humiliating manner. It happens, my friends. When you go through the wilderness, all kinds of things happen.

The first thing that happened – **David was chased out into enemy hands**. Remember Goliath was from Gath. Now David has gone back to the king of the land whose hero he killed. The place you swore never to go, there you are. The enemy that you said you will never meet again in life, you have met him and you are alone. Sometimes, in the wilderness, you are chased into enemy hands. Pressure will push you to places you do not want to be. You will fall into the hands of people who have been looking for you. These are people who have sworn to destroy you and all of a sudden, your friends have pushed you and there you are and you have no way out. So what does David do? He had to do something.

He is challenged with evidence of his first deeds. The people said, "Is this not David, of whom the women swoon, 'David has slain his thousands, and David, ten thousand.'" This is one time where you wish nobody knows you. When you are in the wilderness, you do not want to meet familiar people. People who know your past record that you used to be great, you used to be wonderful and sometimes when you meet them, you want to dodge because life has changed on you and David, I am sure, he has grown a beard because when he killed Goliath, he had no beard. He was just a teenager. Now he has a beard and I am sure he thinks the people will not recognize him, but they make him out, and they say, "Well, that is the man. He is the one who humiliated us some years ago." One day, people are going to use your success against you.

When you are in the wilderness, people take your success and mock you with your success and challenge you with your success and confront you with your success. So when they told David, "Are you not the one who killed Goliath, our brother, our hero, our captain? Are you not the one who was praised some years ago?" David had no alternative but to radically respond to the situation. He was compelled to act in a humiliating manner. I do not know whether you have been there where you have been compelled to act in a way that you never thought you will act. You meet somebody who was your small boy and now you are saluting him, "Yes Sir! Yes Sir!!" Because you have to salute him and your soul hates it, but that is the only way to survive. If you do not do it, you will be killed sometimes, you know, it is heart breaking to see somebody who used to sit at the king's table, now alone and begging for bread and seeking somebody's help.

David, at that time, spat on his own beard, started scratching at doors, making sounds like an insane person and he did it so well that the king actually believed he was insane and the only reason that the king did not kill him was because he thought David was of no further threat to his kingdom. He behaved so well as a madman that the king could not see any potential recovery. He was totally gone. The king could not see any potential of recovery because if he saw any potential of recovery, he would have killed him. David had to convince the king that he has no future. He had to do it so well that the king believed, "This guy will no longer be a threat." So he says, "Get him out of my presence" but that was his salvation because when you are in the wilderness, it is not the time for pride and arrogance.

If you want to show off your pride, you will say, "Yeah, I am the one they sang ten thousand praises to. What do you say?" At that time, David did not boast, could not be proud and could not be arrogant. Sometimes people go through the wilderness experience and still are proud, arrogant and they never learn any lesson. They get destroyed permanently, but David understood in emergency times there are emergency actions. In critical times, there are critical responses. That does not mean, "Go and sin. Go and do something evil." No. David did not sin. He just simply lowered himself to the lowest level so that nobody will consider him a threat any longer.

When he did that, he was cast off with mockery and ridicule. I am sure when he was off, when David was going, he could hear people laughing at him from behind. Have you ever been in a situation where you know that people are laughing at you? It is like going to your alma mater school where you meet old school mates and here you are, with your old dilapidated car (that is if you have one) and you park it far away to make sure nobody sees your car. Go to the meeting with people who have BMWs, Mercedes Benz, Jaguars and 4 Wheel drives; you enter with your old trouser, your shirt is frayed – the blue color has turned into white, the collar is frayed. Your hair is unkempt. Your shoe is seeking for attention so it has opened its mouth crying for help. There you are, you go to the meeting and you are trying so hard to be normal, talking to people, "Chale, long time no see." You are having fun.

At the end of the meeting, people say, "Let us go and see you out." You make every excuse, "Oh, do not worry. I can go by myself." They still insist, "Oh, let us go! Let us go!!" They go up the hill and there is your car because you parked it up the hill so you can push it for it to ignite and there you were up the hill and you sit in your car and your friends turn back, you can see their shoulders shaking and you know they are laughing at you. They are making fun of you and you know for the next few years, you will be topic number one whenever the school meets. That is what happened to David. When he left, he knew for the next few months, the new story in Gath will not be David who killed his ten thousand, but David, the madman and people will say, "Ah, did you see his beard? Did you see the spit? Did you see how he was scratching?" People will make fun of him, but that was a wilderness experience.

The third thing is that in the wilderness with all of these happening God will not abandon you. **He will give you the opportunity for you to prove your calling.** So there is proof of calling. David had this opportunity in Chapter 22 of 1 Samuel verses 1 to 2. He has been humiliated. He is alone, but God is still with him and somehow in close wilderness experiences and moments. God has a way of reminding you that He has not thrown you away.

"This is like fresh water in the desert. This is like good news from a distant land. David therefore departed from there and escaped to the cave of Adullam after he had been mocked. So when his brothers and all his father's house heard it, they went down there to him. And everyone who was in distress, everyone who was in debt and everyone who was discontented gathered to him so he became captain over them and there were about four hundred men with him."(1 Samuel 22:1-2).

In the desert, when the people had departed from him, David gained new support. The wilderness experience is not forever. God will bring new people to you. God will gather a new force around you. He will bring you support. He will bring you people, people to encourage you and there are three groups of people that came to David.

First was **his family**. He received emotional support. Emotional encouragement from his family.

Second were **the dissenters**. Dissenters are people who say that they do not agree with something that other people agree with or that is official policy. Everybody who was in trouble. They came to David. They gave him military strength.

Third, if you read the verse 5, **a prophet came to him and he gave him spiritual guidance.**

Thus, emotional support, military strength for him and spiritual guidance. He gained new support. Is it not amazing that you are in a wilderness experience when everybody you knew has abandoned you, all of a sudden, new people come into your life, and they encourage you emotionally and they make you feel good and people come who can identify with you? All the people who are in trouble like you come around you. The Bible says, "Everybody who was in debt. Everybody who was a dissenter, everybody who was discontented." They saw a person who represented their interests and they gathered for you. He became captain over them.

The first time in his wilderness experience he has an opportunity to lead an army, he did not borrow from Saul. He is building his own army. It is not the best team, but he has something to work with because in the wilderness, God will give you something to work with. He will give you new opportunities in the wilderness and David now has new opportunity.

In the midst of all the humiliation and loneliness, a door of opportunity has opened, but the people that gather around him are nowhere like the people he used to lead. I am sure in the previous army, everybody had their uniform ironed, they had shiny boots, had a nice, military cap. They could take instructions to salute properly. They could go in a precision march, but this new army, people did not know how to march, how to salute. You say, "Eyes right" and they are thinking of where to turn. They have no idea, but they have been running away. They are in debt. The IRS is chasing them from town. So they are also hiding in the wilderness. They have no military experience. They have nothing. They are the rough bunch but that is where he has to start from. That is the good thing about God. He will always send you the seed of the fruit. He wants you to cultivate. God will not give you the fruit. He will give you the seed and out of the seed, you produce your fruit.

In the wilderness, do not expect that everything will work out well. God is not going to solve your problems altogether for you, but He will give you what it takes to solve the problem. He will not give you the end product. He will give you the raw material that you will use to produce your desired vision. He gives you the raw material. God is the God of the raw material. David has people, but they are people like him, whom he has to transform into the people of God – the army that God promised you to have in Jesus' Name. Amen.

People in His image who must become people in God's image. People who look like Him who must become the people of God. God gives you your kind in order to transform into His land. If you do not get used to the fact that what you used to enjoy in the palace was not yours, then you will always quarrel with your own army when they show up because when you were in the palace, you were taking care of someone's army; he has bought a uniform for them. They look nice and you are just there commanding, "Everybody… do this" and they run after you.

You say, "Well, it is my army." No, it is not your army. You just found them "cooked." Now you have the opportunity to build your army and it is the raw material. They do not know how doing anything. If you are not careful and you still retain palace mentality when you are given the raw material, you rebel because you would say, "This is not what I asked for." David had to work with that team. It happens in every situation – in pasturing for instance, God promises you. He has called you and you hear all kinds of prophecies, "Mansa, you are my daughter. I have called you. I will do great things with you. You will change the nations. You will serve the nations."

You hear all the nice prophecies. Prophecy is very sweet. So far I have not seen people who have bad prophecies. "I am the Lord! I am the Lord!!", says the Lord, "I will raise you! I will lift you. You will go to America. Your church will be big. You will be great. You will be a millionaire." You say, "Yes, Lord! Yes, Lord!! Thank you Jesus! Thank you Jesus!!" That is good. The hearing part is good. Then God gives you the raw material. You say, "What is that? This is not my American congregation."

In the wilderness, God will give you the raw material. If you know how to build, build this one. If you know how to do it, there you are. If you have the ministry and if you have the ability, then build that army, grow that army, turn that army into the vision that God wants you to have. If you believe you are going to build a skyscraper, start from the kiosk. Some of us are talking about big things and we are hoping that in the wilderness, one day, a miracle will happen that will solve our problems. I am telling you that you are in a wrong wilderness because in this wilderness you are in, a miracle will not happen. You will have an army of discontented people, people who have no vision, people who have no clue, have no sense of direction. You have to take time and begin to pump, vision into them and guide them, structure them, build them up and format them to produce the results you are looking for.

You know the reason why a lot of people stay in the wilderness for a long time? It is because they were looking for already made solutions and if you are doing that, you will stay in that place for a very long time. They were looking for already made solutions. Sometimes pastors start a church and they get discouraged. I have been to places where pastors complain, "Look at my church. We are poor. Look at where we are." If you wait enough, that seed is going to bear fruit. When you are in the wilderness, God will not give you the finished product. He will give you what you need to start and that is what David had – a ragtag army.

An army of dissidence, confused, unmotivated, uninspired, lack of vision, depressed people and all of them say, "David, we are for you! David, we are for you!!" You look at these people and you wonder, "They should go somewhere." "We are on your side, David." To fully understand this group, you have to understand one day, when they went out and came back, their home had been ransacked, they decided to kill David because these people, they put their destinies into his hand, and they want solutions.

David was now not able to provide the solutions and the Bible says, "The people thought of stoning him to death." "David started crying," says the Bible, "and David encouraged himself in the Lord." Your wilderness experience has a way out, but that way is not paved with gold. It is sometimes paved with rocks and stones and pits and discouragement and tears and frustration, but you have to walk that road out of the wilderness. You have to take what God has given to you and pour your intestines into it.

Pour everything in you into it. No laziness. No half-heartedness. No waiting for somebody to help you. You attack the job with your life. Many of us want solutions, but you do not want to commit hundred percent into it. All of a sudden, we want to fold our legs and give instruction, "You, bring that." It does not happen. When you are in the wilderness, there is no pride. You do not say, "I am the senior pastor of this church. This is my card" and print complimentary cards. It is not the time to post and recognition.

This is the time to invest your energy in the works. Sweat into the soil, your blood into the soil. Not sitting down and looking for accolades and for people to sing your praises because people used to sing, "Saul has killed his thousands and you have your ten thousand." Where is Saul, and where are the thousands? They all have left you. Now this is what you have. You have to learn to work hard in the wilderness because if you obey God, in the wilderness, He will bring you out and take you to the next level because once you start getting out of the wilderness, you are getting close to the throne because it is the process of wilderness that prepares you finally for all the steps you need to take to get to your vision and where God wants to take you.

If you are a king in the making as you read this manuscript, I want you to know the experience you are having is not strange. Some of you, used to work in places. You resign to start your own business and now everything is gone bad. You thought when you started your business, it will be a continuation of your previous employment. In your previous employment, you were sitting in an air-conditioned office, you had a desk, a computer and the secretary. "Secretary, coffee." When you are in the wilderness, you just realize you did not buy the computer you were using. You did not buy the air conditioner. You were not paying the bills so you have no air conditioner and no secretary and if you have a secretary, it is not like that one you call at the palace. She comes, "Boss, wabre? Edwuma yi eden."

You look at your secretary, feeling like firing her, "I will fire you. Wose gya?" You look at the circumstance and you realize, "This is not where I came from." There is no computer, no desk for you to put your feet on, no secretary to dictate to, now you have to type your own letters and file your own files and carry your own bag, drive your own car, sweat in your own room but that is the way you build your own army not Saul's army.

May God give you the strength, the fortitude, the courage, the commitment to stay and build your own work, your own vision until it has become the thing that God promised you to have in Jesus' Name. Amen.

CHAPTER FIVE – DEALING WITH ENEMIES

We are looking at the life of David and how he progressed into leadership as king over Israel, and we have looked at various facts of life – how he was chosen, we looked at the big challenge – Goliath and how he solved that problem for his nation. We looked at how he came into the palace and then we looked at how he went from the palace to the wilderness.

In this chapter, I am looking at how David dealt with his enemies. As God prepares you and raises you up into your throne or into the place that He has assigned for you to be, you are going to have enemies. The world is so full of enemies you do not need to pray for them. They will show up anyway and in the process of rising to the place you belong, you are going to have enough people who will fight you, who will resist you and who will try to destroy you. The kind of response you give to your enemy will determine the character of your leadership. Between you and your throne, there will be enemies, but you have to learn to respond to them rightly.

Before I delve into the story of David, let me just introduce something that Jesus taught in Matthew 13:24-28 because it would give us a context within which to deal with the story of David. Note the words of Jesus very keenly.

"Another parable, He put forth to them saying, 'The Kingdom of Heaven is like a man who sowed good seed in his field but while men slept, his enemy came and sowed tears among the wheat and went his way. But when the grain has sprouted and produced the crop, the tears also appeared. So the servants of the owner came and said to him, 'Sir, did you not sow good seed in your field? How then does it have tears?' He said to them, 'An enemy has done this.' The servants said to him, 'Do you want us then to go and gather them up?' " (Matthew 13:24-28).

Note the phrase of the master, "An enemy has done this." In the process of God elevating you and raising you up to the place you belong, there will be enemies in your life and the harm they cause to you is not what they do against you. That is not the problem. It is what they plant inside you and sometimes enemies can plant seeds, tears in our lives that disturb the great things that God has prepared us to have. I will give you four kinds of tears that enemies can sow into your life and I want you to watch out for them because as we look at the life of David, we will see how he dealt with these systems.

The first one that an enemy can plant in your life is intimidation. When you have faced too many enemies in the world, you start feeling intimidated. You fear, you withdraw, you are constantly on the defense. Intimidation.

The second thing that an enemy can plant in your harvest field, inside your heart is persecution complex. Enemies can sometimes make you feel threatened all the time, so that even when there are no enemies, you think there are enemies; you suspect everybody. You do not trust anybody. You always feel somebody is planning for your destruction. It is the work of your enemy and there are people who have that.

The third is bitterness. An enemy can help to plant bitterness in your heart.

The fourth is vengeance. Watch out for these four seeds that the enemy can have in your life. Do you know that there are some people who rise in leadership and the first thing they do as leaders is to start destroying other people. The first thing they start doing is vengeance. Some are so full of bitterness. Some are so full of persecution complex, they have the power, but they do not trust anybody and some feel intimidated and it is because whiles they were rising into leadership, people attacked them, people fought them and built these systems and then they become leaders and begin to reproduce them so instead of doing the work they are supposed to do, they go about looking for enemies to destroy.

You have to be careful whiles you are surrounded by enemies, so they do not plant intimidation, persecution complex, bitterness and vengeance in your heart. As the master said, "It is the enemy who does these things." How did David respond to his enemies? They could make him feel intimidated. If you are talking about persecution, nobody was more persecuted than David. How did he deal with persecution complex? How come he was able to deal with bitterness? How come he did not spend all his reign on vengeance? Let us look at the life of David closely and see his response to the same circumstances that all of us are facing. 1 Samuel 24:1-22. You are going to have enemies, my friends. How many of you do not have enemies? So who is the enemy? We are all enemies.

Somebody is your enemy and you are somebody's enemy. So there are enemies. Whiles you are unknown, there will be enemies. There are people who fight me and I guess there are people I fight. There are people who do not like me. There are people who plan my destruction. There are people who set traps for me. Whiles I was growing up as a young man, trying to do the will of God, there were people who tried to frustrate every step I took and I guess everyone has a similar story. That means we do it to one another.

Let us see how David dealt with his enemies and at this time, his chief enemy is the king of Israel, Saul, his father-in-law. Can you imagine your enemy is your relative?

"Now it happened when Saul had returned from following the Philistines, that it was told him, saying, 'Take note. David is in the wilderness of. Then Saul took three thousand chosen men from all Israel and went to seek David and David and his men on the rocks of the wild goats. So he came to the sheepfold by the road where there was a cave and Saul went in to attend to his needs. David and his men were staying in the recesses of the cave. Then the men of

David said to him, 'This is the day of which the Lord said to you, 'Behold, I will deliver your enemy into your hand that you may do with him as you seem good to you.' And David rose and secretly cut a corner of Saul's robe.

"Now it happened that afterwards David's heart troubled him because he had cut Saul's robe and he said to his men, 'The Lord forbid that I should do this thing to my master, the Lord's anointed to stretch out my hand against him, seeing he is the anointed of the Lord.' So David restrained his servants with these words and did not allow them to rise against Saul. And Saul got out of the cave and went on his way. David arose afterward out of the cave and called out to Saul, saying, 'My Lord, the king.' And when Saul looked behind him, David stooped with his face to the ground and bowed down. And David said to Saul, 'Why do you listen to the words of men who say, 'Indeed, David seeks your harm. Look, this day, your eyes have seen that the Lord delivered you today into my hand in the cave and someone urged me to kill you, but my eyes spared you and I said, 'I will not stretch out my hand against my lord for he is the Lord's anointed. Moreover, my father, see, yes, see, the corner of your robe in my hand. For in that I cut that corner of your robe and did not kill you, know and see that there is neither evil nor rebellion in my hand and I have not sinned against you yet you hunt my life to take it. Let the Lord judge between you and me, and let the Lord avenge me on you, but my hand shall not be against you.'

"As the proverb of the ancient says, 'Wickedness proceeds from the wicked' but my hand shall not be against you. After whom has the king of Israel come out? Whom do you pursue, a dead dog? A flea? Therefore let the Lord be judged between you and me and see and plead my case and deliver me out of your hand. So it was. When David had finished speaking those words to Saul, that Saul said, 'Is this your voice, my son, David?' and Saul lifted up his voice and wept, 'You are more righteous than I for you have rewarded me with good, whereas I have rewarded you with evil and you have shown this day that you have dealt well with me.

"For when the Lord delivered me into your hand, you did not kill me. For if a man finds his enemy, will he let him get away safely? Therefore, may the Lord reward you with good for what you have done to me this day. Now I know indeed that you shall surely be king and that the kingdom of Israel shall be established in your hand. Therefore swear now to me by the Lord you will not cut off my descendants after me and that you will not destroy my name from my father's house.' So David swore to Saul, and Saul went home but David and his men went up to the stronghold."

This was not the last encounter. Saul, later changed his mind and pursued him again and David spared him the second time. What was it about this young man that made him react differently from what almost all of us will react to? There is something about David that made God look at him and say, "This is a man after my heart. He has problems, but his attitude is right."

In the process of you ascending to your throne, rising to the place God has appointed for you, there will be people who hate you and for some reason, you will have opportunity to pay them back and the way to respond to that opportunity will determine your attitude when you get to the throne. Either you are going to be a bitter, vengeful person or a person who rules, who guides, and who directs with honor. Do you know that in our homes, in our offices, even in churches, there are leaders whose number one job is to seek out for enemies they made before they got to where they are? That is all they are doing. They sit in the office plotting to destroy people who hurt them.

Sometimes, the company is not doing well, but they do not care. All they want to do is to get rid of somebody who pursued them into a cave. Sometimes in churches, sometimes in schools, wherever we are, we have leaders who have allowed their enemies to poison their spirits and then they have lost the ability to lead properly. There are four things about David and how he responded to the opportunity to kill his enemy.

The first thing is that David rejected premature promotion. There will be people who will want to get to where you want to get to before you are ready to get there and sometimes, you yourself will want to get a place before you are ready to get there. It is called premature promotion. When you do not have the maturity to handle the responsibility at hand. At this time, in David's life, yes, he was great. Yes, he was anointed. Yes, he had killed Goliath, but he did not have all the skills necessary to handle the responsibility of the king of Israel. He understood that there was going to be a process that will mature him to handle his future role.

How could he do it? He did not twist prophecy to his advantage. There had been prophecy that God will make David king. There had been prophecy that God will defeat his enemy and now his friends come and quote the prophecy back to him. They said, "This is what God spoke about. He said He will deliver your enemies into your hand." Now the prophecy has come to pass, but David understood that although there is such a prophecy, its fulfillment is not this day. If you are going to be a leader who functionally operates the way God wants you to function, you have to learn to resist the twisting of words and prophecy especially people in the ministry.

If you are a young pastor who is doing well and then people come and quote all kinds of prophecy that God has spoken about your life and every step, they tell you, "This is it. Step out. Be bold. Be brazen. God has spoken." They make you feel the pressure, spiritual pressure to act and if you are not careful, you will run out prematurely into a place God has not called you to. David did not twist prophecy to his advantage.

Secondly, **David opposed popular pressure to take the kingdom by force.** The pressure was coming from his people, from his army. "The king is in your hand. Take it.

The kingdom is yours. After all, God says it is yours. After all, you have been anointed for it. Now you have the opportunity. Take it." He opposed popular pressure.

Thirdly, **he stopped his followers from attacking the king.** Sometimes, you yourself may not attack, but your followers will. Do you know followers are most of the time more zealous than leaders? There are people in church who hate people the pastor does not hate because they think the people are the pastor's enemies. Somebody may hear something, "You cannot say that about my pastor" and want to destroy the person without even consulting the pastor. So followers can sometimes fight battles that you do not want them to fight. Sometimes the follower can be your husband or your wife or your friends, your brothers, your sisters or your colleagues who decide to fight and destroy something because they think the person is fighting the pastor. David's followers were going to kill the king.

You have to understand most of the time, when you are dealing with followers, you are afraid. First, you want their loyalty; you do not want to disappoint them and so sometimes you do not want to tell them, "Do not do it" because you feel if you stop them, you will lose their loyalty and they will not be that faithful. Sometimes you allow them to do the excess, but David stopped those people and said, "You cannot touch this man. Not in my presence. This is not the time. This is not how it is going to happen. If God intends for it to happen, it is going to happen and it will be beautiful in our sight when it happens. It is not going to be dirty. It is not going to be destructive." He rejects premature promotion.

On your way to wherever God is taking you, reject the premature promotion. I have had opportunity similar to what David has had and sometimes when your enemy falls into your hand, it is sweet. Has your enemy fallen in your hand before? The person who is fighting you and you are now part of the board to interview him or his file is before you and here is the one who tried to destroy you and now you have the chance or the one who is delaying your promotion and then the chairman of the board, calls you to ask you about your opinion of the Managing Director. You roll your sleeves. "The day the Lord spoke has come. This time for him to smell pepper."

How are you going to deal with it? Are you now going to start reading all the files unearthing all the files and all his secrets and how he is squandering money and embezzling funds; he has been flirting with the girls in the office and just "smash" because it is your time? That is the easy way. Kill him and take his throne. Destroy him and take his throne, but remember the seeds you sow will germinate. Your throne will never be stable and David understood that. He understood that whatsoever a man sows, that also will he reap. So he rejected premature promotion.

Fourthly, another major thing he did was **he respected divine order**. David understood that though he was anointed king, he was not yet king. The king was Saul.

David was a king in the making. Saul was the king on the throne so far as Saul was on the throne, he could be a person that nobody respects, but as far as David was concerned, that is the order. He respected divine order. Many of us do not respect order. We do not respect authority. We do not respect the system that is established and we fight simply because we disagree and want to tear down, pull down as quickly as possible because it will accelerate our elevation. He respected divine order. How do we see that?

When he cut the corner of Saul's garment, the Bible says, "He felt remorse for cutting Saul's garment." He did not touch the man's flesh. He just cut his garment and yet his heart smote him. Do you know why his heart smote him? The garment of the king was his authority, his office, his vesture. When he wore that garment, everybody knew he was a king. When David cut that garment, it was as if he was reducing the authority of Saul. It was as if he was "cutting" his kingdom from him. He was tearing apart his kingdom from him and although he did it without intention, he just wanted something as evidence. The moment he did it, the meaning, the implication of what he had done struck him and something said, "David, you should not have done that."

He did not kill the man. He just wanted evidence so that the man could see that he had the chance to kill him, but even with his good intention, he realized he had done something he should not have done. He understood the symbolism, the meaning, the implication of his actions. He understood, "If you wrote this letter, this was the meaning." He understood if he made this comment about Saul, this was the meaning. He was cutting it into pieces, although that was not his intention. The meaning dawned on him. How many times have you destroyed something and you did not even feel what you have destroyed?

The hand that feeds you, how many times have you bitten it and did not know you are biting it? You say, "Well, but he is also troubling me. I will also bite. One-one draw." Remember, he is going off. You are coming on. Do you want to inherit his liabilities or you want to go out there in honor and dignity? He felt remorse.

Fifthly, **he honored the office of the king**. He called him, "The Lord's anointed." It is very easy to call a good man "the Lord's anointed" because he is good, but this is a man with a rather unpalatable story about his behavior in the palace. One time, he even went naked in a frenzy and David knew that he had also been anointed. Samuel had anointed him and Samuel, who had anointed Saul said, "The kingdom is taken from Saul and is now given to David." All that had been said, but David said, "This is the Lord's anointed." David understood at this point in time this is the king and he must be respected with the office he holds.

Do not destroy an office you hope to occupy. Do not diminish the value of a position you are trying to get to. Do not destroy your Managing Director, the head of your institution, simply because he is getting on your nerves because if you reduce his office and you will get there, you will sit in a reduced office. The forces, the powers, you take away from will not be given to you when you get there. That is why people start, complaining and fighting for a position, then they get there, the people down there start fighting them because they want the same thing that the other was enjoying. "Why? Why?? We are suffering. The man is driving an air conditioned car. Who does he think he is?" we talk in a frenzy.

Then one day, you occupy the position, you realize it is "hot" and you need some air conditioning, but you have reduced, diminished the dignity of the office. Now you cannot claim what you necessarily need and when you try to get it, they will not agree. So David, although he knew the man was against him, he did not diminish the office of the king. He honored the office. David still regarded Saul as the legitimate leader. He still did and David humbly waited for his set time. He believed there was a time for him and that time was going to come in just as much as the sun sets in the night, it will rise again from the East in the morning.

He knew the time was coming and when you know your time is coming, you are not afraid of what happens around you because you know your time is coming. He knew it. He will be king God has spoken. He actually knew if God said he would be king, he would not be killed before he became king because Samuel had prophesied nobody could kill him so in a sense he had an assurance that his life would be protected because he was in covenant with God. He was supposed to be the next king. So he was pleased to wait for his set time.

If you are impatient concerning where you are going, it is an expression of lack of faith in what you are doing because if you believe it is yours, you will not be impatient. You can wait.

Thirdly, **David refrained from vengeance**. That big word. It influences so many actions. As a matter of fact, the code of vengeance is the code that runs through a lot of civilizations and their actions. You attack me, I attack you. You kill my father, I kill your father. You kill my son, I kill your son. When the sons are finished, you start killing the daughters because somebody killed your daughter. After some time, there is nobody to kill. We have cleared everybody off the streets. You do me, I do you and for us, it is not "you do me, I do you"; it is you do me, I do you more.

You hit me, I hit you twice. You bite me, I bite you thrice so an eye for an eye, a tooth for a tooth. You take my eye for taking yours. We are both blind and happy. It is called vengeance and if anybody had a case for vengeance, David had. The man had been wrongly treated. He took his life into his hands - fought Goliath. He was promised a wife, then the wife was taken away from him and given to another person just to provoke him. Then he was given the second best. He says, "Ok." He will take the wife. Then the king planned with his daughter to kill David and everywhere he went, he was being harassed.

He has gone through depression, humiliation, at a point he has to behave like a madman and he is running non-stop and he is scattered all over. He has no place of certainty. When you are that frustrated, you want to pay back the one who has messed up your life. Many of us are waiting to get the opportunity to show somebody. Like we say in Ghana, "You wait and see. When I get there, you will see." Vengeance. **David refrained from vengeance**. How did he do that? **He spared the king's life**. What had happened was that David was running and in his running non-stop, he went to hide in a cave with his army, his troop; they were hiding in the cave, deep in the cave. That was their hide out. That was their stronghold, just running away from Saul. Now when you hide in a cave for a long time, your eyes get used to the darkness and so he was hiding; his eyes are used to the darkness – he knows his way in and out of the cave because he had been going in and out of the cave. He knows every corner of the cave. Then one day, he is in the cave; it is his stronghold. He knows how to operate from that cave and then right from the entrance of the cave, he sees a shadow of a man coming.

The man is coming alone with only one person because his army cannot take him where he is going. The Bible says, "He was going to take care of his needs." There were no water closets in those days, so he had to take care of his needs. The king is very vulnerable. His stomach is worrying him. He goes to the cave and you do not go to the cave with an army because this is a private matter. I am sure his servant with him stops somewhere and the king goes to a corner of the cave to take care of his needs. Whiles he is in that vulnerable state alone with nobody and not in a position to rise to fight, David had his chance. David saw everything that was happening and he says, "This is the man who has been running after me." His servants say, "Yeah, yeah. Look at him, too, squatting there."

David was watching and he was debating, "What do I do?" his friends are saying, "Get him. Kill him. This is it. God has given him to your hand. There is nobody here. He cannot be defended. We are many. We can kill him and that will be the end of your suffering, running around and leaving your wife and children behind. We will all go back to Jerusalem. You will be king and I will be Minister of Defense." It seemed very easy because the man is vulnerable. He is David's hands, but he spared his life. May God give you the grace to spare the life of your enemies when he puts them into your hand. May the spirit of vengeance never be in your heart. May you be able to look at that person who has hated you all his life and spare him. He will not repent, but spare him because Saul never repented. Sparing him does not mean he will have an immediate change of mind and a recovery of mind. He spared the king's life.

He trusted God to give him justice. He said to the king, "As for me, I have sworn, 'My hand will not touch you because I know you are going down by yourself. You have annoyed God enough. Samuel has prophesied that you are going down, but it will not be by my hand.' So he said, 'I am not going to touch you.' he trusted God to give him justice. He said, "Let God judge between you and me and if God thinks you are just, let Him, bless you; if He thinks I am just, let Him bless me but I cannot trust yourself to touch you. He trusted God. Can you trust God to be your judge? Can you trust God to give you justice? Can you trust God to fight your battles for you? Can you trust God to fight for you and deliver you and protect you? Can you?

Not only did he trust God for justice, **he believed in God for his protection.**

He committed Saul to the Lord. He said, "It is out of my hand, king. Now you are in God's Hands. Whatever God wants to do with you that is up to Him, but me, I will not touch you. I pray you have that spirit to be able to look into the face of the one who is troubling you and tell the person, "As for me, I will not touch you. It is up to God. When you behave that way, people think you are stupid. They think they are foolish. Sometimes they even think you are weak.

The military men of David, thought, "This guy, is he really that strong? Is he afraid? What is it about Saul that he is afraid of? Who is he? Why is he afraid?" David was not afraid of Saul. David was afraid of his destiny and he did not want to start ruling with liability on his head. He did not want to set the wrong tone for the time when God promotes him. So he left him go. People may think you are stupid. That is their problem. That is fine. Let them think what they want to. They may think you are weak, but as for you, make a commitment that your hand will not destroy somebody because he has hunted you that. You have to make that choice, that decision because if you do not pass that test, when God lifts you up, you will always be remembered by the harm you caused in your past.

No matter what you achieve, somebody is going to say, "...But he killed Mr. Jones. But he did that. He stole the throne. But he killed people before he took the throne." Nobody will ever give you the credit that you deserve.

Fourthly, **David reaffirmed loyalty to the king.** The most touching thing for me in this whole scenario is when David cut that piece of garment from Saul's kingly robe and allowed Saul to go out of the cave. Obviously, David used another exit because he knew the cave. He gets up, goes to another high mountain nearby and holds the cloth in his hands and bows to the ground. He is not exalting, "Hey. Hey look. Look." No. it is almost as if he does not want to do it, but he has to do it and he is trying to do it right, with all the decency in his heart. He bows and calls the king, "My father. Look. I am here. I am holding your garment in my hands. I could have killed you. I just want you to know I have nothing in my heart against you." It is loyalty. Support.

For some people, even when they spare you, they will publish in the newspaper, advertisers' announcement, "Jr Kuffour spares his enemies just for you to know the largeness of my heart. I want you to know I could have killed you, but I spared you. Next time be warned!" That was not David's attitude. He was not gloating. He was not exalting himself. He was not using it as a point to use against the king. He did not go and announce to everybody, "Hey. Look. Look. Look. I could have killed him, but I did not. Support me." No. He was very humble about it. When God gives you victory, may you be humble about it and may you never publish your accomplishments to your own promotion because if God wants to promote you, He will promote you. **He reaffirmed loyalty to the king.**

He called him, "My father." He called him, "The Lord's anointed." He used the most respectable respectful language for him and because he did that, he obtained the full commendation of Saul. It is almost as if the man who has been fighting you writes a testimonial about you and is full of praise. David comported himself so well that Saul had no alternative but to confirm prophecy concerning David. He said to David, "You are more righteous than I am. You have rewarded me with good. When a man finds his enemy, he should kill him, but you have not killed him. Now I know you will be king." Can you imagine that? The man who is trying to destroy you now confirms your destiny. May God use your enemy to confirm your destiny.

Then Saul asks for almost the impossible. He says, "I know you will be the king. I know you will sit on the throne. Everything shows. The people love you. God's anointing is upon you. You are behaving yourself wisely. You are not making mistakes. When you come to your throne, remember me, remember my name and my descendants. Do not come to the throne and change everything I did and blot my name out and change the books and rewrite." So now you go to the building dedicated by Saul and you chisel Saul's name out. "Dedicated by..." You put your name there. He says, "What is mine, do not take my name off. Do not kill my descendants. You will be king." David swore before the Lord and said, "As long as I live, whatever is due you, will be yours and your descendants will not suffer because of me."

David promised to protect not only Saul's descendants, but also the name of Saul. Do you know that many times when God allows you to inherit your enemy you blot out his name? You do not want anyone to remember he existed. You do not want anyone to remember he ever did something. If you go to the office, it is like a pastor takes off another pastor in another church brutally through spiritual and non-spiritual means to change everything. The choir's name is may be Voices of Praise; you change it and call it Triumphant Voices. You change everything because this is his time. He wants to obliterate the name of whoever was there but David never did that. As a matter of fact, if you remember, when David heard that Saul had died, he started crying. He said, "How are the mighty fallen?" Do not publish it. God, do not let the daughters of Philistine hear. Then he says to Israel, "Remember Saul, who clothed you with purple." Saul did not do much, but David in his memorial of Saul, said, "Remember him. He did some good things for you. David vowed to Saul, "I do not need your record to make my record good. I will make my own record. So I will keep your record for you and I will also do what I have to do."

Remember when two people came and started boasting, "Oh David, Saul is dead. This is the day the Lord has made. Your enemies will be destroyed." David asked, "How do you know Saul is dead?" "We were there; we killed him ourselves." They hoped to get promotion. David said, "You did what?" The men said, "We killed him! We killed him!! We have solved your problem." David said, "What? Do you know I could have solved it this way, if I wanted to? I was afraid to touch the Lord's anointed and you were not afraid."

He told his guards, "These people do not deserve to live. Get rid of them." What would you have done? What will you do to the one who comes to report bad news about your enemy to you? Promote him? Give him some money? David said, "I do not want to hear that again." As a matter of fact, when David was made king, another son of Saul, was made king called Ishbosheth and later on Ishbohseth was killed, some people came to report David and said, "Now the throne is free and we killed the man ourselves." David said, "What?" He got rid of them too and he showed to Israel that you do not get to the throne through bloodshed. You do it the way God has ordained it to be done and when your time comes and you get there, nobody can stop you. He reaffirmed loyalty to the king.

Psalm 57, I call it David's song in the cave. It was written by David when he was in the cave. You will know what he was talking about when he was in the cave. The Bible describes the psalm as a **Michtam of David** when he fled from Saul into the cave. **A Michtam** is a song, but a song of value. It is a song of worship that deeply expresses the value of the singer to God. When David was in the cave before Saul entered, this was what he was doing. He was not planning to take the kingdom. Listen to his words in the cave. He says:

"Be merciful to me, O God. Be merciful to me. For my soul trusts in you and in the shadow of Your wings, I will make my refuge until these calamities have passed by. I will cry out to God Most High. To God who performs all things for me. He shall send from Heaven and save me. He reproaches the one who will swallow me up, sailor. God shall send forth His mercy and His truth. My soul is among lions. I lie among the sons of men who has set on fire, whose teeth are spears and arrows and their tongue a sharp sword.

"Be exalted above the Heavens. Let your glory be above the earth. They have prepared a net for my steps. My soul is bowed down. They have dug a pit for me in the midst of it, they themselves have fallen, sailor. My spirit, my heart is steadfast in God. My heart is steadfast. I will sing and give praise. Awake, my glory. Awake, lute and harp. I will awaken the dawn. I will praise you, O Lord amongst the people. I will sing to You among the nations for Your mercies reach onto the Heavens and Your truth unto the clouds.

"Be exalted, O Lord above the Heavens. Let your glory be above all the earth." (Psalm 57).

That is what he was singing in the cave and in marches Saul, his enemy. Just as you learn to worship God and praise Him and lift up His name in the midst of calamity, He fights your battles for you. He rises and fights your battles for you. May the Lord fight for you and May the Lord give you a heart of David to deal kindly with your enemy when he falls into your hand. Amen.

CHAPTER SIX – FACING SETBACKS

I believe God is bringing you to kingship and queen ship (for the ladies). God is bringing you to a place of leadership, a place of prominence, a place of honor, and a place of dignity. He is bringing into fulfillment His promises towards your life.

What is a setback? A setback is anything that sets you back. Anything that pushes you backwards. You are trying to advance, to move on, and to get along with your life and all of a sudden something hits you and you begin to go backwards, stop in your progress and so you are not able to move with the same intensity you used to move. That is what a setback is all about.

As God works with you and raises you up into leadership, you are going to face several situations. This chapter is about how David managed setbacks. Your life is not going to be smooth. There may come times and there will come times when you will suffer setbacks and the way you deal with the setbacks will determine whether you are ready for true leadership or not.

"Now it happened when David and his men came to Ziklag on the third day that the Amalekites had invaded the south, attacked Ziklag and burnt it with fire and had taken captive the women and those who were there, from small to great. They did not kill anyone but carried them away and went their way.

"David and his men came to the city and there it was burnt with fire and their wives and their sons and their daughters had been taken captive. Then David and the people who were with him lifted up their voices and wept until there was no more power to weep and David's two wives, Ahinoam and Abigail had been taken captive. Now David was greatly distressed for the people spoke of stoning him, because the soul of the people was grieved; every man for his sons and his daughters.

"But David strengthened himself in the Lord, his God. Then David said to Abiathar, the priest, Ahimelech's son, 'Please bring the ephod here to me.' And Abiathar brought the ephod to David so David inquired of the Lord saying, 'Shall I pursue this troop? Shall I overtake them?' And He answered him, 'Pursue for you shall surely overtake them and without fail, recover all.'

"So David went, he and six hundred men who were with him and came to the brook Besor where those stayed who were left behind." (1 Samuel 30:1-9).

The path of a leader is sometimes, most times beset with setbacks and discouragements – situations that push the person who is seeking to advance. There are times in our lives, when things just get out of joint. Our plans do not happen the way we expect them when things we do not expect happened. That was what happened to David.

He had been in the wilderness for a period now. He was trying hard to make a living for himself. He has the army of the men and their families with him. They built a small city to build their houses there. They bought property, furniture.

Everybody was happy with what they had achieved. They were in the wilderness, but life was beginning to make sense to them. They had their wives, their children with them and things were beginning to work for them.

Then all of a sudden out of nowhere, out of the blue, there is an attack on their town and everything is lost. Properties are burnt and stolen. Wives and children are taken captive. There are times in our lives where we work so hard for something and we believe "This is it. This is our future." We put so much confidence in it and then all of a sudden it is gone. What do you do when you have worked so hard, but lose what you have worked for as you make your progress to be what God wants you to be?

That was the situation of David. His town was invaded, attacked, burnt and his people were taken captive. I am going to take you through seven steps in relating to your setbacks or facing your setbacks and I am going to pull each one of them from David's attitude and if you want to be a leader, you cannot avoid problems, but your attitude in times of difficulty will show whether you have the character of a leader or the character of a quitter because leaders do not quit. They persist, they progress and they move on with their lives, even in the face of insurmountable adversities. So what did David do when he came upon this situation, when everything was gone? His people had lost everything they had worked for, David himself, had lost everything he had worked for.

David shared the sense of loss and defeat with his people. His people had lost. He had lost. The Bible says, "When they came upon the situation, the leader, David could not just look on and pretend to be immune to the problems." Sometimes when you are a leader, even when you are suffering, you pretend as if you are not suffering, but David came upon the situation and his people started crying and he also started crying. A leader and his followers were all crying. They shared their sense of loss together. It is important to understand when you are growing as a leader that you are not a Superman neither are you a Superwoman that when you come through difficult moments of your life, you do not have to pretend as if it is nothing.

When the problem is actually affecting you and pitching you, you have to be like David. You should be able to share your sense of grief. You should be able to express emotionally your loss. His people had lost, he had lost and they shared their sense of loss together. They had lost valuable property and people. They had lost wives, children, houses, furniture, jewelry, clothes; things they have worked for. David rightly mourned and wept.

The Bible says, "He and his people wept so much that there was no more power in them to weep." Have you ever come to that point when you weep and all your tears are finished? You weep out every reservoir of tears inside you and you weep so hard you cannot weep again. We used to go through those moments when we were children. Probably, your mother spanked you (which was very normal). Then you went and hid in a corner and started crying.

After some time your tears were dried up and your energy to weep was gone so you began to sob deeply. Did you ever do that? That was where David was. Tears were gone. He could not cry any longer. He was deeply sobbing. Sometimes when you are in such a situation, you have wept out all your tears, people may think you are pretending

CHAPTER SEVEN – ON THE THRONE

At this time of year many people will have been going to nativity plays in churches and schools. Many people will think briefly upon the impact of the birth and life of Jesus Christ. Many will sing, read and hear about how the baby born in Bethlehem was to be a great King but few will understand its true significance or the scope of what this truly means. In this chapter, we take a quick look at the true meaning of the kingship of Christ and his purpose in God's plan for the earth.

Christ – "the King of the Jews"

"Now when Jesus was born in Bethlehem of Judaea in the days of Herod the king, behold, there came wise men from the east to Jerusalem, Saying, Where is he that is born King of the Jews? For we have seen his star in the east, and are come to worship him." Matthew 2:2

We see here that Jesus Christ was born to be the King of the Jews. The wise men from the east were awaiting his birth – probably from the teachings of the Jewish prophet Daniel who, although captured and taken to Babylon, rose through the ranks to become an important and influential figure in the Babylonian empire which was situated to the east of Israel. Jesus Christ though was never accepted by the Jewish nation as their king. When they crucified him they were angry with Pilot for his words which were placed at the top of the cross:

"And Pilate wrote a title, and put it on the cross. And the writing was, JESUS OF NAZARETH THE KING OF THE JEWS. This title then read many of the Jews: for the place where Jesus was crucified was nigh to the city: and it was written in Hebrew, and Greek, and Latin. Then said the chief priests of the Jews to Pilate, Write not, The King of the Jews; but that he said, I am King of the Jews." John 19:19-21

Did Jesus Christ fail then if he was born to be *'King of the Jews'*? No He did not as we shall see.

The Angels Message to Mary

The well-known words of the angel to Mary hold some profound prophetic words:

"And the angel said unto her, Fear not, Mary: for thou hast found favour with God. And, behold, thou shalt conceive in thy womb, and bring forth a son, and shalt call his name JESUS. He shall be great, and shall be called the Son of the Highest: and the Lord God shall give unto him the throne of his father David: And he shall reign over the house of Jacob forever; and of his kingdom there shall be no end." Luke 1:30-33

We have here then a prophecy that Jesus Christ would be given the *"throne of his father David"*. We read that when this throne is given to him his kingdom shall have *"no end"*. What does this mean?

The Kingdom of God in the Past – the *'throne of David'*

To understand the prophecy of the angel an understanding of the Old Testament must be obtained. God's kingdom was in fact the ancient Kingdom of Israel. We can see this from the following passages of scripture:

The nation of Israel were God's *"kingdom"* and he was their *"king"* allowing them to inhabit *"His land"* – the land of Israel (see Isaiah 43:15, 44:6 , Exodus 19:5-6, Psalm 114:1-2, Ezekiel 36:5).

Israel eventually wanted a man to be their king (1 Sam 8:7). These kings were only ruling on behalf of God (2 Chronicles 9:8).

In Chronicles we read King David's words:

"And of all my sons, (for the LORD hath given me many sons,) he hath chosen Solomon my son to sit upon the throne of the kingdom of the LORD over Israel." (1 Chronicles 28:5)

David and his son Solomon were therefore rulers of the *'Kingdom of God'* in the past.

These facts serve as a key which unlocks major parts of the New Testament as we shall start to see as we continue.

The Kingdom of God Temporally Overturned

In Ezekiel we read a prophecy against the last of the line of the Kings of this Kingdom. This is what God said to king Zedekiah:

"...and thou, profane wicked prince of Israel, whose day is come, when iniquity shall have an end, Thus saith the Lord GOD;

Remove the diadem, and take off the crown: this shall not be the same: exalt him that is low, and abase him that is high. I will overturn, overturn, overturn, it: and it shall be no more, until he come whose right it is; and I will give it him." Ezekiel 21:25-27

So we see that the Kingdom of God was only to be overturned for a limited time *"until he comes whose right it is"*. There is then to be a *'coming one'* who will have the *'kingdom'* given to him – that Kingdom which King David of old sat on a throne governing.

There are plenty of prophecies in the Old Testament about the future revival of this past Kingdom. Consider these:

"And in mercy shall the throne be established: and he shall sit upon it in truth in the tabernacle of David, judging, and seeking judgment, and hasting righteousness." Isaiah 16:5

"In that day will I raise up the tabernacle of David that is fallen, and close up the breaches thereof; and I will raise up his ruins, and I will build it as in the days of old:" Amos 9:11

"And the LORD shall inherit Judah his portion in the holy land, and shall choose Jerusalem again." Zechariah 2:12

The message to Mary unlocked

With that Old Testament background we can revisit and better understand that message from the angel to Mary. Remember it was said of Christ that:

"...and the Lord God shall give unto him the throne of his father David" Luke 1:32

This was the ancient throne of the Kingdom of Israel which was over throne as we saw in Ezekiel 21:27. That throne that King David of old sat on. A throne which governed a literal territory on earth. That throne is to be given to Jesus Christ and when it is given to him it will last forever. This was indeed promised to King David.

"And when thy days be fulfilled, and thou shalt sleep with thy fathers, I will set up thy seed after thee, which shall proceed out of thy bowels, and I will establish his kingdom. He shall build an house for my name, and I will establish the throne of his kingdom forever... And thine house and thy kingdom shall be established for ever before thee: thy throne shall be established forever." 2 Samuel 7:12-17

So this seed would do these things *"before David"* (a resurrection from the dead) and that this future descendant would reign forever (e.g. be immortal!). The New Testament opens with words which hint at this:

"The book of the generation of Jesus Christ, the son of David, the son of Abraham." Matthew 1:1

We see then the importance of understanding who David was and the fact that Jesus Christ was his descendant and therefore heir to the throne of the Kingdom of God in the past.

We read in the angel's message to Mary:

"...he shall reign over the house of Jacob forever" Luke 1:33

This links in with the promise to David. The *"house of Jacob"* is a term which simply means the descendants of Jacob. Jacobs name was changed to Israel in the Bible and he is the father of the Jewish nation. So this king will specifically be the *"King of the Jews"* and rule over the ancient but literal Kingdom of Israel just as King David of old did.

When does Christ become King?

Some people believe that Jesus is a king now but he has not been yet given the throne of the Kingdom of Israel. He is currently set down at the right hand of Gods throne which is different to the throne which will be set up when Jesus finally is given it upon the earth (see Rev 3:21 for proof that there are two distinct thrones in this respect). Jesus has not yet restored the Kingdom to Israel yet as we can see when the apostles asked him this question:

"When they therefore were come together, they asked of him, saying, Lord, wilt thou at this time restore again the kingdom to Israel?" Acts 1:6

This question was asked after the death and resurrection of Christ and proves that it was their earnest expectation that the Kingdom of Israel would once again be restored with Jesus Christ as King. However 'then was not the time' for Jesus replies:

"And he said unto them, It is not for you to know the times or the seasons, which the Father hath put in his own power." Acts 1:7

The return of Christ to establish God's Kingdom

The great message of the Bible is that Jesus will return from heaven to establish the Kingdom of Israel. This was the promise of the angels to those apostles who saw Jesus go to heaven. This is what they said to them:

"...while they (the apostles) looked steadfastly toward heaven as he went up, behold, two men stood by them in white apparel; which also said, Ye men of Galilee, why stand ye gazing up into heaven? This same Jesus, which is taken up from you into heaven, shall so come in like manner as ye have seen him go into heaven." Acts 1:10-11

So Jesus is to return to restore this Kingdom which will eventually grow and take over the whole earth (see Daniel 2). This Kingdom will be like the Kingdom of God in the past, it will have a righteous King (Christ) a Capital city (Jerusalem or Zion), a law etc. and its influence will grow until all nations have come into subjection to it. We read of this in various places but here are a few passages to consider:

"And in the days of these kings shall the God of heaven set up a kingdom, which shall never be destroyed: and the kingdom shall not be left to other people, but it shall break in pieces and consume all these kingdoms, and it shall stand for ever." Daniel 2:44

"They shall call Jerusalem the throne of the Lord; and all nations shall be gathered unto it; neither shall they walk any more after the imagination of their evil heart." Jer. 3:17

"And I will make... her that was cast far off a strong nation: and the LORD shall reign over them in mount Zion from henceforth, even for ever. And thou, O tower of the flock, the strong hold of the daughter of Zion, unto thee shall it come, even the first dominion; the kingdom shall come to the daughter of Jerusalem." Micah 4:7-8

The Kingdom of God in the past then will be re-established with Christ as its king – but at this future time ALL nations will be in subjection to it. This Kingdom will bring peace to the earth and all peoples will know about God and want to please Him. We are given a few glimpses in the Bible of what this wonderful kingdom on earth will be like:

There will be such benefits for its citizens such as have never been seen before:

A peaceful safe existence (Isaiah 2:4, 32:17, 65:21-22, Zechariah 8:4-5)

A *"righteous"* system of justice (Isaiah 11:3-4, 32:1)

Good health and long life (Isaiah 35:5,6, 65:20)

A healthy earth which will produce an abundance of food (Joel 3:18, Amos 9:13, Psalm 72:16, Zechariah 8:12, Isaiah 35:1, Ezekiel 36:34-35)

In this amazing Kingdom we are told that *"...the earth shall be full of the knowledge of the LORD, as the waters cover the sea."* Isaiah 11:9

Your part in God's Kingdom

The Bible holds within it a wonderful message of hope. It offers you and I a chance to be part of this future Kingdom which Christ is coming to establish. When one understands the gospel message which contains the *"things concerning the kingdom of God"* and the *"name of Jesus Christ"* and is baptized (Acts 8:12) this opens the way to a place in that Kingdom on earth.

How different the message of the Bible is then with what most people associate with Christianity and the birth of Christ. His birth was miraculous and amazing and we have only looked at one aspect of Christ role in Gods purpose. However we hope we have shown you that there is more to this subject then stories. There is more to it than what even the churches around proclaim. We encourage you to pick up your Bible and read it, and discover it is true and wonderful message for yourself. Why leave Jesus in the manger until the following year? Get to know him and his purpose through Gods word, the Bible.

The promise to David

The promise to David is the third of the great promises made by God upon which all further revelations are based. This promise is essential if one it to understand the Bible and especially if one is to appreciate what the Bible teaches about Jesus Christ.

Background to David's life

David was a divinely nominated King of Israel and described in the scriptures as *"a man after God's own heart"* (1 Samuel 13:14). Although he was not perfect he had an amazing faith in God and desired to see God glorified above all else.

David, by conquest had extended the Kingdom of Israel to its greatest extent and God had given King David *"rest from his enemies"* and had made his house to prosper. In light of this David wanted to build a temple for the worship of God.

In response to this God told him, through the prophet Nathan that He would not allow him to build the temple but his son, Solomon would. However God promised David that He would actually build David a house and this promise, along with its details forms another foundation promise of the gospel. The most significant part of this promise is that the seed of David would sit upon his throne, as king, ruling over an everlasting Kingdom. This is in fact the further unfolding of a previous promise God gave to Abraham:

"In the same day the LORD made a covenant with Abram, saying, Unto thy seed have I given this land, from the river of Egypt unto the great river, the river Euphrates:" Genesis 15-18

The promised seed (descendant) therefore is connected with the land of Israel.

Why is this important?

If you study what the Bible says about Jesus, you will note that there are lots of references to King David and the promises made to him. Jesus is to fulfill these promises and therefore to understand them is to appreciate what God's purpose through Jesus Christ is. Consider the following:

"For unto us a child is born, unto us a son is given: and the government shall be upon his shoulder: and his name shall be called Wonderful, Counsellor, The mighty God, The everlasting Father, The Prince of Peace. Of the increase of his government and peace there shall be no end, **upon the throne of David***, and upon his kingdom, to order it, and to establish it with judgment and with justice from henceforth even forever. The zeal of the LORD of hosts will perform this." Isaiah 9:6-7*

"And when he had removed him, he raised up unto them David to be their king; to whom also he gave testimony, and said, I have found David the son of Jesse, a man after mine own heart, which shall fulfil all my will. Of **this man's seed** *hath God according to his promise raised unto Israel a Saviour, Jesus:" Acts 13:22-23*

"I Jesus have sent mine angel to testify unto you these things in the churches. I am the root and the offspring **of David***, and the bright and morning star." Revelation 22:16*

What was promised to David?

The promise to David is recorded in 2 Samuel 7. Its different aspects have been defined below:

- Israel, God's chosen people, would eventually settle and would be safe (this is yet to be fulfilled!) – 2 Samuel 7:10

- The promised seed would be a descendant of David – 2 Samuel 7:12

- This seed (or descendant) would build a house for God – 2 Samuel 7:13

- God, as well as David would be the seed's Father – he would be the *"Son of God"* – 2 Samuel 7:14

- God's mercy would remain with David's seed – 2 Samuel 7:14-15

- David's throne an Kingdom is to be established FOREVER – 2 Samuel 7:13-16

- The throne and the seed would be done *"before"* David (e.g. in front of him) – 2 Samuel 7:26

What does this mean?

This covenant has not yet been fulfilled. Jesus was the seed (descendant) of David who was to come. Here are two references in the gospels to prove this:

*"He (Jesus) shall be great, and shall be called the Son of the Highest: and the Lord God shall give unto him the **throne of his father David**: And he shall reign over the house of Jacob forever; and of his kingdom there shall be no end".* Luke 1:32-33

*"The book of the generation of Jesus Christ, the **son of David**, the son of Abraham".* Matthew 1:1

So Christ then was the descendant (or seed) of David but also he was the son of God as was promised to David:

"And the angel answered and said unto her, The Holy Ghost shall come upon thee, and the power of the Highest shall overshadow thee: therefore also that holy thing which shall be born of thee shall be called the Son of God". Luke 1:35

The promise stated that David would see his descendant (Christ) sitting on his throne, the throne of David in Jerusalem and that his Kingdom would continue forever. This is to happen in the future when Jesus Christ returns to the earth to establish that kingdom.

"And we declare unto you glad tidings, how that the promise which was made unto the fathers, God hath fulfilled the same unto us their children, in that he hath raised up Jesus again... And as concerning that he raised him up from the dead, now no more to return to corruption, he said on this wise, I will give you the sure **mercies of David**". Acts 13:32-34

David himself realized that this covenant would be fulfilled through one greater than himself and he spoke of this in one of his Psalms which the apostle Paul later picks up on:

"My covenant will I not break, nor alter the thing that is gone out of my lips. Once have I sworn by my holiness that I will not lie **unto David**. *His seed shall endure forever, and his throne as the sun before me. It shall be established for ever as the moon, and as a faithful witness in heaven"*. Psalm 89:34-37

"THE LORD hath sworn in truth **unto David**; he will not turn from it; Of the fruit of thy body will I set upon thy **throne**." Psalm 132:11

"THE LORD (God) said unto my Lord (David's seed), Sit thou at my right hand, until I make thine enemies thy footstool". Psalm 110:1

"Men and brethren, let me freely speak unto you of the patriarch **David**, that he is both dead and buried, and his sepulcre is with us unto this day. Therefore being a prophet, and knowing that God had sworn with an oath to him, that of the fruit of his loins, according to the flesh, he would raise up Christ to sit on his throne; He seeing this before spoke of the resurrection of Christ, that his soul was not left in hell, neither his flesh did see corruption. This Jesus hath God raised up, whereof we all are witnesses. Therefore being by the right hand of God exalted, and having received of the Father the promise of the Holy Ghost, he hath shed forth this, which ye now see and hear. For David is not ascended into the heavens: but he saith himself, The LORD said unto my Lord, Sit thou on my right hand, Until I make thy foes thy footstool. Therefore let all the house of Israel know assuredly, that God hath made that same Jesus, whom ye have crucified, both Lord and Christ". Acts 2:29-36

Clearly then, the Bible teaches that David must be resurrected, that Jesus Christ must come back to the earth to sit upon David's and set up a Kingdom which will last forever. This will be a re-establishment of the Kingdom of

God (over which David ruled). God told the last king, King Zedekiah, this:

"Thus saith the Lord GOD; Remove the diadem, and take off the crown… I will overturn, overturn, overturn, it (The Kingdom of Israel): and it shall be no more, until he (Jesus Christ) come whose right it is; and I will give it him". Ezekiel 21:26-27

So this Kingdom then is to be re-established in the future. The one who is to come of whom God will give the Kingdom is Jesus Christ, the descendant of David and son of God.

"Behold, the days come, saith THE LORD, that I will perform that good thing which I have promised unto the house of Israel and to the house of Judah. In those days, and at that time, will I cause the Branch of righteousness to grow up **unto David***; and he shall execute judgment and righteousness in the land. In those days shall Judah be saved, and Jerusalem shall dwell safely: and this is the name wherewith she shall be called, The LORD our righteousness. For thus saith THE LORD; David shall never want a man to sit upon the throne of the house of Israel". Jeremiah 33:14-17*

In Hebrews 11 we have a list of faithful followers of God. David is mentioned in verse 32. We also read in that chapter the following:

"And these all, having obtained a good report through faith, received not the promise: God having provided some better thing for us, that they without us should not be made perfect." Hebrews 11:39-40

So then these promises are in the future and we can be associated with them by belief in them, being baptized and following a faithful life. Peter tells us that by having a knowledge of these things that there have been:

"...given unto us exceeding great and precious promises: that by these ye might be partakers of the divine nature, having escaped the corruption that is in the world through lust". 2 Peter 1:4

"The LORD has sworn to David. A truth from which He will not turn back; of the fruit of your body I will set upon your throne." (Psalm 132:11). The Psalm from which this statement is taken is of a group of Psalms that were used in worship at the temple of God at Jerusalem. They were each called *"A Song of Ascent"* and this one asks for the Lord to bless the sanctuary, or temple, sometimes referred to as "Zion" after the mount upon which it was built in Jerusalem.

But this Psalm is also prophetic in nature, referring to a promise the Lord had made to David through the prophet Nathan years before. The promise had involved the establishment of a permanent king who would sit down on the throne of David forever. This king would be a descendant of David.

Where do we look for the fulfilment of this promise? Has it been fulfilled as yet, or is it something to be fulfilled in the future? Many look for a future fulfilment in which Jesus will come back to literal Zion and rule from Jerusalem on David's throne.

Nathan's Prophecy Concerning David's throne

[From the LORD through His prophet Nathan to King David] *"When your days are complete and you lie down with your fathers I will raise up your descendant after you, who shall come forth from you, and I will establish his kingdom. He shall build a house for My name, and I will establish the throne of His kingdom forever. I will be a father to him and he will be a son to Me when he commits iniquity, I will correct him with the rod of men and the strokes of the sons of men, but My loving-kindness will not depart from him, as I look it away from Saul, whom I removed before you. And your house and your kingdom shall endure before Me forever; your throne shall be established forever."* (2 Samuel 7:12-16)

This prophecy at first presents an interesting question, *"Is this prophecy about David's descendant Solomon or about his later descendant Jesus?"* The answer must be: *"BOTH!"*

Building the Lord's House (vs. 3). In one sense, it is Solomon who built the Lord's House when he built the temple at Jerusalem. But Jesus also built a House for God; made of living stones, a spiritual temple; the church of Christ (1 Corinthians 3:16-17; Ephesians 2:19-22; 1 Peter 2:4-5).

The establishment of the descendant's kingdom (vs. 12). The Lord did establish Solomon's kingdom. Under Solomon, the kingdom of Israel prospered, reaching its zenith. But the physical kingdom of Israel was not established forever as it does not exist today. However, it did give birth to God's spiritual kingdom. Jesus established this kingdom (Mark 9:1; John 18:36; Colossians 1:13) and it is indeed eternal and *"cannot be shaken."* (Hebrews 12:22-29).

Iniquity and correction (vs. 14). Solomon did fall away for a time. The Lord did correct him and he came back to God. Some of the most thought-provoking writings of the wise man Solomon are made about his mistakes and what he learned from them. However Jesus had no sin Himself (Hebrews 4:15). But He did suffer correction *"with the rods of men," "strokes of the sons of men"* for our sins. He bore our sins on the cross, paving the way for our redemption (Isaiah 53; 2 Corinthians 5:21).

In either case, whether Solomon or Jesus, we find that Nathan's prophecy has indeed been fulfilled. This is not a prophecy about a kingdom yet to be established in our future when Jesus comes again. King Jesus is already reigning over His kingdom (Revelations 1:5, 9).

How the Prophecy Has Been Fulfilled

"Brethren, I may confidently say to you regarding the patriarch David that He both died and was buried and His tomb is with us to this day. And so, because he was a prophet, and knew that God has sworn to him with an oath to seat one of his descendants upon his throne, he looked ahead and spoke of the resurrection of Christ, that He was neither abandoned to Hades, nor did His flesh suffer decay. This Jesus God raised up again to which we are all witnesses. Therefore, having been exalted to the right hand of God, He has poured forth this which you both see and hear" (Acts 2:29-33). According to the Holy Spirit,

communication through Peter and the apostles, the promise to *"seat one of David's descendants upon this throne"* was fulfilled by the resurrection and exaltation of the Lord Jesus to the right hand of God. *"Therefore, let all the house of Israel know for certain that God has made Him both Lord and Christ – this Jesus whom you crucified."* (vs. 36).

The Hebrew writer refers to Nathan's prophecy as being fulfilled as well; *"For to which of the angels did He say, 'Thou art My Son, Today I have begotten Thee?' "* and again, *'I will be a Father to him and He shall be a Son to Me?' "* and *"But of the Son is forever and ever, and the righteous scepter is the scepter of His kingdom."* (Hebrews 1:5-8).

Putting It All Together

"Truly I say to you, there are some of those who are standing here who shall not taste death until they see the Son of Man coming in His Kingdom." (Matthew 16:28). Jesus said this in the 1st century. Jesus said that those living in the 1st century would be *"see the Son of Man coming in His Kingdom."* The Kingdom of Jesus had already been in existence in the 1st century following His death, burial and resurrection. Jesus Himself had explained that the Kingdom which He would establish in the 1st century was spiritual in nature, and we find that men and women who subjected themselves to His race were made partakers in His spiritual kingdom.

We have seen that Jesus has sat down on David's spiritual throne, ruling over spiritual Zion, a kingdom which cannot be shaken but wait. The Hebrew writer in one of the passages already cited (Hebrews 12:22-29) talks of the final destruction of the physical heaven and earth (vs. 26, 27). What will happen to this eternal kingdom of which we believers are a part when the final hour has passed? How will it continue to stand when the very cosmos is removed from existence?

The answer is that Jesus is coming again. When He comes, the citizens of His kingdom shall rise, bodies changed to that which is spiritual, immortal and incorruptible. Then Jesus will gather His Kingdom together and take us home. You see, He is not coming again to establish His Kingdom, but to deliver it up to the Father (1 Corinthians 15:23-26).

Also Available By Benjamin Osei Kuffour Jnr.

Available Everywhere Books are sold.

www.ingramcontent.com/pod-product-compliance
Lightning Source LLC
Chambersburg PA
CBHW070108080526